Book of Edward
Christian Mythology

Volume IV

Appendixes—Reference

Why will some Christians actually go to Hell? If you are a Christian, this book may save your eternal soul and the eternal souls of your family. Who is Jesus talking about when he said: "I never knew you" in Matthew 7:21-23? Christians! So, which Christians have broken the covenant of Jesus' blood on the cross? Why are they headed to Hell instead of Heaven? The answers are inside.

The Apostle Edward

Introduction

Book of Edward
Christian Mythology

Copyright © 2005 by Edward G. Palmer
Published by JVED Publishing
Elk River, Minnesota 55330

> ISBN 0-9768833-3-3 (Volume IV: Appendixes—Reference)
> ISBN 0-9768833-4-1 (4 Volume Set)

Palmer, Edward G.
    1. Faith—The Apostle Edward   2. Bible Prophecy—Christian Mythology
    3. Christianity—Christology

Printed in the United States of America.

All rights reserved. No portion of this book may be reproduced in any form without the written permission of the Author.

Notice. This book and its entire contents represents the sole opinion of Edward G. Palmer based upon his twenty-five plus years of in-depth Bible studies, his actual life experiences, his personal diaries and readily available public records. No part of this book is intended to offer professional counseling of any type especially that of legal advice. Persons involved in cultic churches, those in need of spiritual counseling, medical, legal or any other advice should seek competent professional help.

Capitalization Protocol. On all Bible citations, regardless of the translation used, and where the context clearly points to God Almighty or to Jesus Christ, this book makes the distinction between the two by using either small cap characters or lower case characters. For God Almighty, a small capitalized style protocol is followed and reflected in the format: CREATOR, FATHER, GIVER, HE, HIS, HIM, HIMSELF, YOU, YOUR, ME, MINE, MOST HIGH, MY, MYSELF, LORD and SAVIOR, ETC. For Jesus Christ, a lower case protocol is used except for Lord and Son. Hence, when these pronouns are used for Jesus, they show up as: he, his, him, himself, you, your, me, my, myself, savior, Lord, or Son. This has generally been followed throughout the book, but is not the case with every cited verse. It is used for those verses in which the context cannot be easily disputed or in the case of citing a quality or attribute, which belongs solely to God. For those interested in the original translation capitalization, the author refers them to the actual Bible version used for the cited text. A list of Bible translations is shown on the next page. In some other cases, capital letters used within the cited sentence structure were also changed on common words for ease of reading or modern grammar. In other cases, the capitalized letters were left as shown in the original translation. Hence the original Bible phrase "; Because" might appear as "; because." In all instances, Apostle Edward maintains complete integrity of translation and the writings herein can be traced back to the original Bibles to confirm the accuracy of presentation. While not perfect, the capitalization protocol is fairly consistent and enhances the reading and value of Apostle Edward's teachings.

Introduction

Translation Notice

The following Bible translations were researched for this book along with three Hebrew texts and one or more ancient manuscripts such as the Book of Enoch (ENO). Except where otherwise indicated and in regards to capitalization of words, all Scripture quotations are taken from the Holy Bible, New King James Version © 1979, 1980, 1982 by Thomas Nelson, Inc., Publishers. Verses that are followed by a two, three or four-letter capitalized identifier are from the following Bible translations or reference works.

Abbreviation	Bible Definition
KJV; NKJV	King James Bible[1]; New King James Bible[2]
AMP	Amplified Bible[3]
ASB; NASB	American Standard[4]; New American Standard Bible[5]
DB	Darby Bible[6]
ENO	Book of Enoch — Richard Laurence 1883 Edition[7]
GN; GNB	Good News[8]; Good News Apocrypha[9]-Today's English Bible
GW	God's Word Bible[10]
HEB	Hebrew Bible — English Translation JPS 1917 Edition[11]
JSB	Jewish Study Bible[12] - Jewish Publication Society 1985, 1999
LIV; NLT	Living Bible[13]; New Living Translation[14]
MB	MicroBible[15]
MLT	Morris Literal Translation[16]
MOF	James Moffatt Translation, Final Edition[17]
NIV	New International Bible[18]
NCV	New Century Bible[19]
NJB	New Jerusalem Bible[20]
REB	Revised English Bible[21]
RSV; NRSV	Revised Standard Bible[22]; New Revised Standard Bible[23]
SET	Simple English Translation[24]
TAN	Tanach - The Stone Edition 1996[25]
TB	Transliterated Bible[26]
WEB	Webster's Bible[27]
WEY	Weymouth's NT[28]
YLT	Young's Literal Translation[29]

Copyright 2005 Edward G. Palmer, All Rights Reserved.

Introduction

Table of Contents

Page

Dedication vi

Foreword viii

Prophecies Fulfilled x

Volume I
Matters Of The Heart

Chapter 1: It Starts With The Heart 1

Chapter 2: God Speaks To The Heart 11

Chapter 3: Repentance From The Heart 28

Chapter 4: God's Call Of The Heart 59

Chapter 5: Practice From The Heart 72

Chapter 6: The Heart Of An Apostle 93

Chapter 7: Choices From The Heart 131

Volume II
God Does Not Change

Chapter 8: Understanding God's Word 171

Chapter 9: Rationalization of Mankind 204

Chapter 10: The False Trinity Doctrine 242

Chapter 11: God's Eternal Character 312

Chapter 12: The False Salvation Doctrine 382

Chapter 13: A Light On My Path 416

Chapter 14: The Gift of Jesus 452

Copyright 2005 Edward G. Palmer, All Rights Reserved.

Introduction

Volume III
Itching Christian Ears

Chapter 15: Myth — God Heals Everyone 492

Chapter 16: Myth — God Owns Solid Rock 545

Chapter 17: Myth — Giving 10% Is A Tithe 615

Chapter 18: Myth — Abortion Doesn't Matter 678

Chapter 19: Myth — Sexuality Doesn't Matter................................. 749

Chapter 20: Myth — Politics Doesn't Matter 897

Chapter 21: Myth — Everybody Gets To Go 977

Epilogue.. 1039

Volume IV
Appendixes—Reference

Appendix A: A Real Salvation Prayer 1043

Appendix B: Baptism Doctrine 1046

Appendix C: Doctrinal Statement 1049

Appendix D: Jackie's Final Thoughts 1069

Appendix E: Ed's Goodbye Eulogy 1072

Appendix F: Cancer Killing Protocols 1083

Appendix G: Illustrations, Tables & Lists 1092

Appendix H: Notes & Bibliography... 1099

Appendix I: Bible Verse Cross Reference 1134

Appendix J: Index 1177

Dedication

This book is dedicated to my beloved wife Jacqueline Lee (Bowers) Palmer whose love I was privileged to have on this earth for the thirty-nine years of our marriage and the four years of our teen love that preceded it from 1960-1964. On June 3, 2003, God gave Jackie her heavenly wings. This book was started during our thirty-seventh year of marriage and finished in what would have been our fortieth year.

In the forty-three years of earthly love that we shared, God used Jackie to teach me the simplicity of a genuine faith and the resulting earthly righteousness, which is manifested by that faith. Christian mythology has distorted the righteousness message of Jesus Christ. This book sets the record straight again about what it really means to accept God's Son.

Introduction

God also used Dean H. Mattila, Jacqueline Mattila and Vernon Enstad to teach me. They are the three righteous people whom God chose for me, from within the church, to share the spiritual journey of this book with. These three alone had the courage to stand tall for the truth and stand by my side when we left a fellowship of Christians who long ago decided to turn their back on the truth and embrace mythology.

Then there is Michael and Maureen Gill, two righteous people whom God brought into my life uncommitted to Christ at the time and used by God to illustrate as HE did to Peter in Acts 10:34-35 NIV that, "How true it is that God does not show favoritism but accepts men from every nation who fear HIM and do what is right."

Jesus confirms the kingdom requirement of righteousness in Matthew 25:46 with his words: "Then they will go away to eternal punishment, but the righteous to eternal life." In Luke 5:32, Jesus further clarifies this by saying: "I have not come to call the righteous, but sinners to repentance."

This book is also dedicated to the memory of my first son Glen; to daughter Paula & husband James Kantorowicz; daughter Patty & husband Jon Morin; son Brian & wife Brandee Palmer; grandchildren Christopher, Paul, Kathryn, Bradley, Benjamin, Luke, Braiden, Bronson, those yet to arrive and to the memory of grandson Dylan.

This book is also dedicated to the memory of my parents and sister Barbara and all others whom have passed on, to my younger brother James Stanley, his wife Denise and sons Jimmy, John and Nick. This book is also dedicated to Karen and Amy whom God brought into my heart and who will always be like a daughter and granddaughter to me.

Finally, this book is dedicated to the Christian family that my wife and I were raised in. How wonderful to have lived life in a fellowship of people not afraid to talk about the Holy Bible, our God and what it means to have a genuine faith. To those in the family who have wondered why I chose to accept God's calling, the answers will be found in this book. I will always be grateful for all of these special people who shared in my life and I trust that our LORD will find them excellent members of HIS kingdom, even while on this earth and in this present existence. The Apostle Edward

Introduction

Foreword

It was a strange scene for me as I found myself watching television on a recent Sunday morning. As I prepared to leave to open the doors of my own church, I found myself instead surfing with the remote for a few moments. TV is not a high priority for me, but I was interested in seeing what was on the tube in the way of church services. Perhaps for my dear wife who would be taking care of grandkids at home that morning? Perhaps for my grandkids? Perhaps simply for some good content for my own church teachings? It didn't matter.

All of a sudden, I found myself watching the worship service of a church I had heard much about. It was an Assembly of God church in the Minneapolis metro area. The name is not important. What was important to me at the time was what I saw. I was watching a praise and worship service on television and it captivated my spirit. The church was reported by some to be "hot." You know, filled with the Holy Ghost and with signs and wonders. The service was "spirit-filled." I can tell you this by just watching as the people were giving their hearts to God in song, dance, praise and worship.

For years, it was wonderful for me to go up to the altar area, lift my head and arms as high as I could, and praise the LORD. I would sing and dance around the altar getting "drunk" in the Holy Spirit [see Acts 2:15-21]. The object of praise and worship for me was to press into God's Spirit and presence. We are taught in the Bible that through Christ Jesus, we are given the Spirit of truth. We are also taught that it is our ticket to step into the Holy of Holies to be with God.

For me, the worship service was very captivating to watch. I felt myself desiring to "sing, dance, praise and worship" God among those worshippers I saw. The "praise and worship" looked genuine and as my spirit was drawn in further, I sensed my heart crying out: "Make room for me!" There is simply something wonderful worshipping God. We are taught in the Bible that "In HIS presence" is fullness of joy. For me, that is exactly what "praise and worship" is all about—getting into company with HIM. I have never known the level of joy I feel with God in anything of this worldly existence. That isn't to say the world cannot provide you and I with joy. It can, but that kind of joy is short lived. With God, it is always there, it's eternal in nature: you just have to "press-in" to HIM.

Copyright 2005 Edward G. Palmer, All Rights Reserved.

Introduction

As much as I wanted to join the praise and worship service, I couldn't help but wonder: "Who in the crowd was worshipping God in vain?" Who in this particular crowd was going through the motions but inside were not "lovers of the truth?" Who in this particular crowd was still going to Hell yet thinking they were saved? The truth has been perverted from many pulpits and Paul's prophecy in 2 Timothy 4:3-4 was now fulfilled.

You see I recently left a church with this same type of "inviting" praise and worship service. However, Solid Rock Church turned out to be a den of thieves, filled with wicked and unrighteous people [Luke 19:46]. People who consider themselves Christian; yet, who routinely and without much thought ignore the truth. Turning their backs, God saw the fullness of their false witness.

God reminded me of HIS word in Matthew 15:8-9 "These people draw near to ME with their mouth, and honor ME with their lips, but their heart is far from ME, and in vain they worship ME, teaching as doctrines the commandments of men." And again it is written in Mark 7:7 that "They worship ME in vain."

Do you worship God in vain? Many, who call themselves Christians, and who think of them selves as being saved by the blood of Jesus, are simply deluding themselves on the way to their eternal home in Hell. Jesus tells us of this fact. Why? Does it have to be this way?

The message I received from God is to tell those who call themselves Christians that many of them will be going to Hell and that Jesus will serve up a very rude announcement to them as they plead for their eternal soul. However, by that time, it will be too late. So, who are these Christians?

Who is Jesus speaking to in Matthew 7:22-23? Jesus says: "Many will say to me in that day, 'Lord, Lord, have we not prophesied in your name, cast out demons in your name, and done many wonders in your name?' And then I will declare to them, I never knew you; depart from me, you who practice lawlessness." Jesus' message is clearly to those who call themselves Christian. To those who say: "I am saved by the blood of Lamb" or "I know Jesus." This book is a warning to Christians. Many of you are headed to Hell. Why?

The Apostle Edward

Introduction

Mythology Prophecy

"For the time will come when men will not put up with sound doctrine. Instead, to suit their own desires, they will gather around them a great number of teachers to say what their itching ears want to hear. They will turn their ears away from the truth and turn aside to myths."

2 Timothy 4:3-4 NIV

Truth Prophecy

"The coming of the lawless one will be in accordance with the work of Satan displayed in all kinds of counterfeit miracles, signs and wonders, and in every sort of evil that deceives those who are perishing. They perish because they refused to love the truth and so be saved. For this reason God sends them a powerful delusion so that they will believe the lie and so that all will be condemned who have not believed the truth but have delighted in wickedness."

2 Thessalonians 2:9-12 NIV

Prophecies Are Fulfilled

"The prophecies in 2 Timothy 4:3-4 and 2 Thessalonians 2:9-12 are fulfilled. Today, mythology is routinely taught from the pulpits of many Christian churches instead of God's Holy Word and many people attending Christian churches have turned away from the truth. These people are headed toward Hell unaware of their lost souls."

The Apostle Edward

Appendixes-Reference
Volume IV

Book of Edward

Appendix A
A Real Salvation Prayer

OPENING PRAYER: FATHER God, let everyone who utters this prayer of salvation unto YOU, with a sincere heart, immediately feel the presence of YOUR Holy Spirit and equip them with the internal strength of conviction to stand tall for YOUR righteousness at all costs and even unto their own human death. Verily I say unto YOU that this is YOUR expectation of their [my] sincere heart. The Apostle Edward

INSTRUCTIONS: Pray out loud and offer up to God Almighty outstretched arms and the following prayer, on your knees, in the privacy of your prayer closet [private room, alone], and with your sincere heart. Verily I say unto you that your soul will see eternal life in Heaven upon the death of your earthly body if your heart is sincere with God to the point that your behavior turns to righteousness. Mark down the time, date and place of this gift of your heart to God and feel free to share this moment of time when you made a commitment to walk in God's ways with HIS priorities over your life.

PRAY: Heavenly FATHER, the only ONE and True God. YOU, who are also the FATHER and the only ONE and True God of my brother Jesus Christ whom YOU sent down as a living human sacrifice for the sins of all the humans in this earthly realm and world, hear this prayer from my sincere heart. This prayer comes from within the bowels of my spirit-soul and I fully understand that this is a one-way decision of my heart.

A Real Salvation Prayer

FATHER, I believe in YOUR only human begotten Son Jesus Christ. I believe that YOU sent Christ down to this earth and that he became the human being Jesus Christ [Yashua] in the flesh just like the flesh I have. I believe he had bones like I do, flesh like I do and blood like I do. I believe that his body on the cross was no different than any other human body on the cross. I acknowledge Jesus Christ is the Son of God; he is not God.

FATHER, I believe that he only spoke what YOU told him to say and that he only did what YOU told him to do. I believe that he was the final and perfect blood sacrifice for the forgiveness of the sins of mankind. FATHER I believe that includes my sins.

LORD, I fully acknowledge that by accepting Jesus Christ as my personal savior and brother that I am inviting his perfect spirit into my life to share this earthly body with me. Along with his spirit, I understand that you will also give me YOUR Holy Spirit and that YOU also will dwell within me.

I believe that the end result of my sincere acceptance of this gift of YOUR Son is the Oneness that I will share with YOU and him. Christ has taught me that I might live in perfect Oneness, Peace and Joy with YOU and him. O LORD, this is truly the sincere desire of my heart. I no longer want to be spiritually alone.

Therefore, I accept the precious gift of YOUR Son Jesus Christ and I repent of my past sins and sincerely regret every thought, action, behavior or anything that was displeasing unto YOU. I understand that with the precious gift of YOUR Son, YOU expect me to live a righteousness life the rest of my days on this earth.

Such a life entails living up to YOUR expectations and obeying what YOU and YOUR Son taught us in Holy Scripture. LORD, I acknowledge that I cannot be perfect in and of myself. I realize that to be like Christ requires that I "practice" righteousness and that I avoid sin to the best of my ability. I acknowledge that to continue willfully to sin is a tacit rejection of the gift of Jesus.

Copyright 2005 Edward G. Palmer, All Rights Reserved.

Book of Edward—Appendix A

A Real Salvation Prayer

I also acknowledge FATHER that there will be unintentional and unknown sins that will come in my life. I understand that YOU and Christ will cover those types of sin and function as a guide in my life to keep me on the narrow path to Heaven.

FATHER, I acknowledge that YOUR Son is not a free pass on sins like so many Christians believe. Therefore, when I realize I have sinned against YOU in any way, I promise to confess that sin immediately and to keep a short list of my missteps with YOU. I know YOU are faithful to forgive under such conditions, but I also realize that if any life is filled with such confessions that it will be a testimony of an insincere heart. I recognize YOUR instructions in Ezekiel 18 and that Jesus has not altered YOUR criteria for punishing sinners. Therefore, keep me under YOUR wings O God and give me a pure heart unto YOU.

Having said this FATHER, I pray that you will dwell within me and help me to be the man [or woman] that you want me to be. I ask all of this in the name of Jesus Christ whom I confess with my mouth that he came in the flesh as YOUR only begotten SON. I acknowledge with my heart that YOU expect righteousness, a new life with changed behavior; behavior that glorifies YOU.

FATHER, help me to be an instrument of YOUR will even as Christ was such an instrument. Let this day be the first day of the rest of my life and help me to put away all offensive behavior and sin, which YOU hate. In the name of YOUR only begotten and beloved human Son Jesus, I pray. AMEN

Date and Time of Prayer: _____

Place of Prayer: _____

I First Told To: _____

_____

Appendix B
Baptism Doctrine

THE QUESTION

An Internet email writer asks: "What is your doctrine on baptism? Do you believe that it is necessary to be baptized in order to go to Heaven?"

Dear Seeker,

This is a very deep question. I will do my best to answer it faithfully in a way that honors God.

OUR DOCTRINE

I believe in baptism by immersion as an "outward expression of a new heart, which is now set aside for God." In effect, such a water baptism declares to all you know [and to the world] that you are indeed a part of God's kingdom [and you are indeed headed towards a heavenly kingdom].

COMMENTARY & STUDY

In Ephesians 4:5 we read: "There is one Lord, one faith, one baptism." However, in Acts 19:3-4 we see the question posed: "Into what then were you baptized?" The answer: "Into John's baptism." John's baptism was one of "repentance for the remission of sins." See Mark 1:4. Explicit in Acts 19:3-4 is the reality that there was more than one type of baptism.

Baptism Doctrine

John the Baptist offered the proposition of a "real God, Heaven and Hell and thus a real reason for sincere repentance" to the people. It is clear in God's Word that any such sincere repentance [of the heart] would yield salvation or eternal life. Thus baptism, in this instance by John, leads to eternal life in Heaven. John's baptism is not well understood in Christianity, which has perverted the intent of God's Holy Word and the Gospel of Christ.

However, Ephesians 4:5 refers to another and second baptism. It is the baptism of Romans 6:4: "Therefore we were buried with him [Christ Jesus] through baptism into death, that just as Christ was raised from the dead by the glory of the FATHER, even so we should walk in newness of life."

Anyone who accepts Jesus Christ "in their heart" has indeed accepted the reality of God and has achieved a baptism of the Holy Spirit [a baptism unto death and resurrection in Christ]. This results in the indwelling of God, HIS Son and the Spirit of truth that allows you to walk in a "newness of life." It gives you the strength to stand tall, firm and unwavering for God's truth in the simple language of the Holy Bible. Such a person now manifests the kingdom of God from within outward into the world around them. Even though, at this point, there may not have been a water baptism.

Baby baptism means virtually nothing because at the age of accountability [about 12 years old], each individual will have to make his or her choice as to which side he or she is on. No one can make this choice for another soul.

It took 10 years, after God touched my heart, for me to get baptized by immersion. It was a wonderful moment in time for me as it had bothered my spirit for a long time. Perhaps out of the misdirection of Christian theology and not fully understanding God's Holy Word. Or, perhaps out of the desire of my heart to proclaim that "I belong to God." Or, perhaps out of verses like Acts 10:47 indicating I could be baptized "having already received the Holy Spirit" and Acts 8:37 since "I believed with all my heart."

The verse that was my spiritual testimony at the time of my water baptism was Acts 22:15-16: "For you will be HIS witness to all men of what you have seen and heard. 'And now why are you waiting? Arise and be baptized, and wash away your sins, calling on the name of the LORD.' "

Copyright 2005 Edward G. Palmer, All Rights Reserved.

Book of Edward—Appendix B

Baptism Doctrine

And now, why are you waiting? I knew where my heart was and the book of Acts indicated to my spirit that it was a special privilege to get baptized by immersion having met all of God's 'heart' criteria to ... make an outward declaration of the faith that was inside of my heart!

CASE 1: Anyone who is baptized by immersion and repents unto God for his or her sins will be saved and enter into eternal life. Assuming they then walk a godly life. This is true even without them having accepted Christ since they have already "accepted God."

CASE 2: Anyone who accepts Christ accepts God and, if Christ is within them, they will walk in the newness of life through a baptism of the Holy Spirit. This is true even if they have not been water baptized by immersion. Assuming they then walk a godly life and are "truly repentant."

This baptism doctrine fully recognizes all of God's Word. When you study Ezekiel 18, you will understand Case 1. It is consistent with the Gospel of Christ, which is "to repent and be saved." Many Christians no longer have this perspective of repentance. It is a critical part of salvation. Repentance leads to righteousness. Righteous people belong to God!

Case 2 is also consistent with God's Word. God has offered us a different dynamic with HIS Son. Plus, HE has provided some spiritual help that we can internalize through Christ: the indwelling of HIS Holy Spirit abundantly. Case 2 is consistent with Romans 10:9-10, which spells out what is required for salvation through Christ. Water baptism is not a part of the criteria Paul outlined, because his criteria, results in a baptism of your spirit-soul and also a committed heart. As such, you have accepted God's Spirit via Christ. It is a 'Spirit' baptism. Both baptisms require the total surrendering of your heart and life in obedience to God. Do either and HIS Spirit will confirm to your spirit-soul that you are indeed saved unto eternal life.

The Apostle Edward

"THE LORD OUR GOD IS ONE!" Deut 6:4

Copyright 2005 Edward G. Palmer, All Rights Reserved.

Book of Edward

Appendix C
Doctrinal Statement

1. **Christians are those people who have** "established a personal relationship with God [the FATHER]" because of having known Jesus [HIS Son]. Jesus has given us an "understanding of God" [and has brought us back to God]. 1 John 5:20

2. **Real Christians**:
    a. Know God because they know Jesus. John 7:17; 1 John 5:20
    b. Understand that God is a friend. Exodus 33:11; James 2:23; Proverbs 18:24
    c. Talk, dialogue and reason directly with God. Isaiah 1:18
    d. Love God with all their hearts, souls, minds & strength. Mark 12:30
    e. Love God and obey God's commandments. 1 John 5:3; John 14:15
    f. Serve and worship only God [the FATHER]. Matthew 4:10
    g. Worship God [the FATHER] in spirit and in truth. John 4:23
    h. Pray to the FATHER [God] in Heaven. Luke 11:2
    i. No longer ask of Jesus, because Jesus told them to ask of the FATHER. John 16:23
    j. Ask of the FATHER [God] in Jesus' name. "Go direct to God!" John 16:23 LIV
    k. Understand that there is only — ONE God, who is neither a trinity nor Jesus. Mark 12:32
    i. "Yet for us there is ONE God, the FATHER, of whom are all things, and we for HIM, and one Lord Jesus Christ, through whom are all things and through whom we live." 1 Cor. 8:6
    l. Believe that Jesus is the Christ [the human Son of God in the flesh]. 1 John 5:1
    m. Resist sin and are not habitual sinners. 1 John 5:18

Doctrinal Statement

---

n. Practice righteousness. 1 John 2:29
o. Are slaves to righteousness. Romans 6:16-18
p. Purify themselves because Christ was pure. 1 John 3:3
q. Have Jesus Christ as an advocate before God in the event they fail to live up to God's commandments [1 John 2:1]. There are sins that are "unintentional against the commandments of God" [Leviticus 4:2]. There are also "sins that are unknown" [Leviticus 5:17]. Note: Christ fills our gap for these two types of sins.
r. Walk like Jesus walked. I.E. Christians emulate Jesus' character. 1 John 2:6
s. Walk a narrow walk [Matthew 7:13-14]. Walk in the spirit [Romans 8:1].
t. Are doers of the Word and not hearers only, deceiving themselves. James 1:22
u. Understand the kingdom of God is inside them. Luke 17:20-21 Note: As servants of a living God, Christians manifest God's kingdom into the world by their obedience to God's commandments and the actions they take based upon the Word, their faith and God's Spirit's direction.
v. Are filled with the Holy Spirit, which is the Spirit of truth. John 16:13
w. Pray in private to God. Matthew 6:6
x. Are forgiving people. Matthew 6:14
y. Seek justice through proper authorities as taught in Romans 13.
z. Do not testify in a dispute or follow a crowd [leaders] in a way that perverts justice. Exodus 23:2
aa. Do not hide sin. "Purge evil from among you." Deut 13:5; 17:7,12; 19:19; 21:18-21; 22:20-24; 24:7; Judges 20:13 NIV. Note: Instead of living with evil within the Church and society, God has clearly given us instructions to purge the evil from among us. No exceptions.
bb. Are a new creation [key to salvation] in Christ. Galatians 6:15
cc. Are a witness for Christ [that God is true]. Acts 1:8
dd. Get their praise from God as a [real] Jew, not from men. Romans 2:29
ee. Understand that Hell is a real place just like Heaven. Matthew 10:28

Copyright 2005 Edward G. Palmer, All Rights Reserved.

Book of Edward—Appendix C

Doctrinal Statement

---

ff. Understand that "the soul who sins shall die" [Ezekiel 18:4; Luke 13:3; Romans 2:12; Romans 6:23 (wages of sin is death); and, 2 Thess 2:10].

3. **God's commandments are not burdensome.** 1 John 5:3 Note: God expects us to keep all of HIS commandments with a heart that actually fears HIM [Deuteronomy 5:29]. Fear in this situation is exactly what it means. Real fear that a real God actually does exist and will eventually deal with evil and wicked people. Fear is a believer's incentive to "really obey" God. Real Christians have this fear; but their love for God transcends this fear in practical living as "perfect love casts out all fear." 1 John 4:18 "He who fears has not been made perfect in love." When you start to live it, then you will understand it.

   a. "The fear of the LORD [God] is the beginning of wisdom. A good understanding, have all those who do HIS commandments." Psalm 111:10

   b. "Do not fear those who kill the body but cannot kill the soul. But fear HIM [God] who is able to destroy both soul and body in Hell." Jesus in Matthew 10:28

4. **Whoever keeps the commandments is assured of eternal life.** Matthew 19:16-19 "Whoever breaks one of the least of these commandments and teaches men so, shall be called the least in the kingdom of Heaven." Matthew 5:19

   a. Note: Many preachers today teach the idea that God's commandments no longer apply. They are wrong! Scripture teaches us to obey God's commandments.

   b. "All the other commandments and all the demands of the prophets stem from these two laws and are fulfilled if you OBEY them. Keep only these [TWO] and you will find that you are obeying all the others." Matthew 22:40 LIV

5. **People can be righteous with God if they so choose.** "And they [Zacharias & Elizabeth] were both righteous before God, walking in all the commandments and ordinances of the LORD blameless." Luke 1:6

Copyright 2005 Edward G. Palmer, All Rights Reserved.

Book of Edward—Appendix C

Doctrinal Statement

6. **He who practices righteousness is righteous just as Jesus is righteous** [1 John 3:7]. Note: Many Christians have the erroneous idea that they cannot be righteous people. This is poor discernment and shows a lack of real understanding of God's Word.

7. **God has set up a dividing line in history that is at John the Baptist.** Before John, the prophets set down the law. From John, the kingdom of God shall be preached. Luke 16:16 Note: The reason Jesus preached the kingdom of God is to make it real to people. If the kingdom of God is real to you, THEN you will repent and change your ways.

8. **The Gospel of Jesus Christ is: "Repent for the kingdom of God at hand"** [Matthew 4:17]. Further, Jesus taught "I must preach the kingdom of God to other cities also, because for this purpose have I been sent" [Luke 4:43]. The "gospel of the kingdom" will be preached as a witness to all the nations [Matthew 24:14]. Note: Jesus came to reassert God's message of salvation, which existed long before Christ came in the flesh.

9. **Jesus purpose was to preach the kingdom of God.** Luke 4:43

10. **Jesus never equated himself as equal with God [the FATHER].** Instead, Jesus always pointed people back to God [the FATHER]. "Nor is he who is sent [Jesus] greater than [God]..." [John 13:16]. If Jesus were a co-equal with God, Jesus would know everything that God knows. However, in Matthew 24:36, Jesus states: "... only my FATHER [God] knows." Also in Mark 13:32 etal.

    a. Jesus is our high priest in the temple of [Jesus'] God. Rev 3:12

       i. "He who overcomes, I will make him a pillar in the temple of my God." Rev 3:12

       ii. "In all things Jesus had to be made [human] like his brethren, that Jesus might be a merciful and faithful High Priest in things pertaining to God." Heb 2:17 [paraphrased]

       iii. "Jesus is a priest forever according to the order of Melchizedek." Heb 7:21

Copyright 2005 Edward G. Palmer, All Rights Reserved.

Book of Edward—Appendix C

Doctrinal Statement

      iv. Note: Do you go to church to worship the priest? No. Yet, this is exactly what many misled Christians do. They worship Christ the High Priest and messenger when they worship Jesus. He is our High Priest who will lead our worship of God in Heaven. Instead, they should worship God [the FATHER] as Jesus has commanded us to do. John 4:23-24

  b. "Jesus is our brother if we do [God's] will." Matthew 12:50
  c. "Why do you call me good? No one is good but ONE, that is God." Mark 10:18
  d. "I can of myself do nothing." John 5:20
  e. "HE who sent me is true." John 7:28
  f. "I am going back to my FATHER and your FATHER, to my God and your God." John 20:17 NCV
  g. "I do nothing of myself." John 8:28
  h. "I [Jesus] fully obey God." John 8:55 LIV
  i. "I must work the works of HIM [God] who sent me." John 9:4
  j. "My FATHER is greater than all." John 10:29
  k. "The FATHER is greater than I am." John 14:28
  l. "Whoever believes in me is really believing in the ONE who sent me." John 12:44 NCV
  m. "You believe in God, believe also in me [Jesus]." John 14:1
  n. "The FATHER is glorified in the Son." John 14:13
  o. "There is ONE God, the FATHER … [and there is also] one Lord Jesus Christ" 1 Cor 8:6
  p. "[Jesus] has sat down at the right hand of the throne of God." Hebrews 12:2
  q. "Blessing and honor and glory and power be to HIM [God] who sits on the throne *and [also] to the Lamb* [Jesus, who sits to the right of God's throne], forever and ever." Revelation 5:13
  r. "He who overcomes, I will make him a pillar in the temple of my [Jesus'] God and he shall go out no more." Revelations 3:12
  s. "[Jesus is] the beginning of all that God has made." Revelation 3:14 NCV "The beginning of the creation of God." NKJV

Copyright 2005 Edward G. Palmer, All Rights Reserved.

Doctrinal Statement

---

11. **To understand Jesus' teachings, you must understand that he was on this earth to speak for God and that God told Jesus what to say and do. Jesus was obedient to God.** John 8:27, 38

    a. "But as my FATHER taught me, I speak these things." John 8:27 Paraphrased with some discernment, Jesus states: "But as God taught me, I have told you verbatim."

    b. Note: There is much confusion about Jesus' ministry and who he was. However, to understand Jesus simply requires that you read the words of Jesus and pay close attention to them. Many Christians say that John 1:1-3 is proof that Jesus is God in the flesh. Quite the opposite message exists when you read what the Apostles said Jesus spoke along with Jesus' actual words [from God] that he spoke in Revelation chapters 1-3.

12. **To understand John 1:1-3 ["and the Word was God"] you have to understand Revelation 3:14 in that Jesus was the "beginning of all that God has made."** NCV

    a. Note: The Amplified version of Revelation 3:14 reads "the Origin and Beginning and Author of God's creation." Jesus describes himself as "The words of the Amen" in the RSV Bible.

    b. Jesus does not state in Rev 3:14 that he was God. Instead, Jesus states clearly that he was the instrument that God used when God made HIS creation. That is why John 1:3 states, "All things were made through him, and without him nothing was made that was made."

    c. Note: As an exercise in discernment, view John 1:1-3 in NKJV as shown below in D) as written and then paraphrased in E) with the new knowledge that Jesus was: 1) the beginning of all that God has made [Rev 3:14]; 2) an instrument used by God in the rest of the creation [Rev 3:14, John 1:3]; and, 3) that Jesus only spoke those words that were given to him by God to speak [John 8:27, 38].

    d. Written text of John 1:1-3 NKJV: "In the beginning was the WORD, and the WORD was with God, and the WORD was God. He was in the beginning with God. All things were made through him, and without him nothing was made that was made."

Copyright 2005 Edward G. Palmer, All Rights Reserved.

Book of Edward—Appendix C

Doctrinal Statement

    e. Paraphrased: "In the beginning was the Word, and the Word was with God, and the Word was God. [Jesus] was in the beginning with God. All things were made through [Jesus], and without [Jesus] nothing was made that was made."

    f. Comment: The fact that Jesus as the word of God was originally within God does not negate the words of Jesus that testify that he [Jesus] is not God and that Jesus was the "very beginning of God's creations." The first thing that God did was to put HIS Word into HIS first creation [Jesus] — which was then used as an instrument in the rest of God's creation. While this explanation might be controversial to some people, it does not require that you be brain dead by ignoring what Jesus actually did say in the Bible for the sake of getting along with any denomination's man made doctrines on the trinity concept.

13. **The phrase "I and my FATHER are one" in John 10:30 does not mean Jesus is God.**

    a. It is a spiritual analogy like the one Jesus used to explain why a husband and wife were of one flesh. "So then, they are no longer two but one flesh." Matthew 19:5

    b. Likewise, you are not God simply because Jesus said that you, he and the FATHER are "made perfect in one" or that the FATHER and Jesus would make their home with you. You can become ONE flesh with God and Jesus in this same spiritual sense if you choose.

        i. "We will come to [you] and make OUR home with [you]." John 14:23

        ii. "At that day you will know that I am in my FATHER [God], and you in me [Jesus], and I in you." John 14:20 -- This does not make you God, does it?

        iii. "I in them, and YOU in me; that they may be made perfect in ONE" John 17:23

14. **To understand John 14:6 —"I am the way, the truth, and the life. No one comes to the FATHER except through me."** — requires that you observe the rest of what Jesus taught and not read into this scripture more than what the verse actually says.

Copyright 2005 Edward G. Palmer, All Rights Reserved.

Book of Edward—Appendix C

Doctrinal Statement

a. Jesus teaches us that salvation [life] comes from God [the FATHER]. John 5:26

b. Jesus teaches us that God has also granted [life] salvation to him. John 5:26

c. "Salvation belongs to our God who sits on the throne, <u>and</u> to the Lamb." Rev 7:10

d. Jesus teaches that those who believe in God [the FATHER] <u>already have</u> eternal life, will not come into judgment and have passed from death into life. John 5:24.

   i. Jesus confirms his purpose in bringing the people back to God in this verse and states unequivocally that those who believe in God do have eternal life. Nothing here about confessing Jesus as Lord. Only "listening to what Jesus has taught and then believing in God." Jesus contradicts most Christian theology preached today.

e. John 14:6 is Jesus' statement to Thomas that the <u>words from God are the Way to eternal life to those who believe and obey</u>. The statement that no one comes to the FATHER except through Jesus has more to do with a line forming at the right side of Jesus, who sits on the right side of God. Thus, Jesus will be the first to interview and confirm whether he knows you per Matthew 7:21-23. If not, Jesus will then pass you along to God [the FATHER] with a statement like this: "FATHER, I do not know this one, do YOU?" Thus, all who come to the FATHER will really go <u>through</u> Jesus! This will be a part of his selection process [Matt. 7, 25].

f. This is because Jesus' purpose <u>was</u> to preach repentance and bring people back to God. That means there are those who belong to God <u>and</u> those who belong to Jesus. "I [Jesus] came not to call the righteous, but sinners to repentance." Luke 5:32

g. "For the eyes of the God are on the righteous, and HIS ears are open to their prayers." 1 Peter 3:12 paraphrased.

h. "Then Peter opened his mouth and said: 'in truth I perceive that God shows no partiality. But in every nation whoever fears HIM

Book of Edward—Appendix C

Doctrinal Statement

and works righteousness is accepted by HIM.'" Acts 10:34-35
Comment: The righteous already belongs to God Almighty!

  i. "I see very clearly that the Jews are not God's only favorites! In every nation HE has those who worship HIM and do good deeds and are acceptable to HIM." Acts 10:34-35 LIV

15. **To fully understand God and HIS intent for Jesus, you have to understand Jesus' parable of the landowner** in Matthew 21:33-42; Mark 12:1-12; and, in Luke 20:9-19.

    a. The landowner is God and the property is our souls.
    "All souls are MINE." Ezek 18:4

    b. The servants sent by the landowner are the Prophets, God had previously sent.

    c. The Son who ultimately is killed returning for God's property [your soul] is Jesus.

16. **Jesus died for the sins of the world; not so you could now freely sin!** John 3:16

    a. "What shall we say then? Shall we continue in sin that grace may abound? Certainly not! How shall we who died to sin live any longer in it?" Romans 6:1

    b. "Whoever has been born of God does not sin, for HIS seed remains in him; and he cannot sin, because he has been born of God." 1 John 3:9

    c. "In this the children of God and the children of the devil are manifest: Whoever does not practice righteousness [what is right in the eyes of God] is not of God, nor is he who does not love his brother" [1 John 3:10]. Note: Those who continue to willfully sin belong to Satan and not to God.

    d. Note: Many Christians now believe they are free to sin because the blood of Jesus has them covered. Wrong! Romans, Hebrews, 1 John, Ezekiel, Jeremiah and other books of the Bible make it clear that you are responsible for your sins. Continue to willfully sin and you will see death at judgment time, not life.

Copyright 2005 Edward G. Palmer, All Rights Reserved.

Book of Edward—Appendix C

Doctrinal Statement

Jesus has you covered for unintentional and unknown sins against God assuming you actually are trying to live a sin free life.

    e. Jesus says: "Go and sin no more." John 8:11 [See item #29].

17. **"Whoever continues to willfully sin does not have the salvation of Jesus Christ."** Hebrews 10:26

　　a. Note: Can you lose your salvation? The answer is yes. You could say it is an issue of not being a real Christian, as "real Christians" cannot lose their salvation. However, this is a lack of spiritual discernment. Read Revelations 1-3 and note how many times Jesus admonishes you to "hang in there." If you cannot lose salvation, why is Jesus telling you that you can? Faith is a one-way street with God and the Word teaches that it is better for those who never knew God than for those who turn away from God after knowing HIM. It would be if they never knew HIM. Yes, salvation can be lost and this fact is plain in God's Word. In addition to Hebrews 10 and Revelations chapters 1-3, study Ezek chapter 18.

18. **"You will find God when you search with all your heart and soul."** See Deut 4:29 and Jeremiah 29:13. Note: All your heart and soul means you <u>want</u> to love God more than you love everyone else or anything else in life [including wealth]. It means you place God above your spouse and children, work, world, riches, etc. It does not mean you do not love your family. Quite the contrary. As you love God and draw near to HIM, HE will increase the love you have for your family. Your capacity for love grows as HE fills you to overflowing with HIS love.

　　a. "Draw near to God and HE will draw near to you." James 4:8

19. **Jesus made it clear that those who belong to him — actually do obey him.**

　　a. "So why do you call me Lord when you won't obey me?" Luke 6:46 LIV

　　b. "If anyone keeps my word he shall never taste death." John 8:52

Copyright 2005 Edward G. Palmer, All Rights Reserved.

Book of Edward—Appendix C

Doctrinal Statement

20. **Many Christians are going to Hell because Jesus "never knew them."** Matthew 7:21-23 — *Note: They never obeyed him!*

21. **Abortion is evil and unacceptable in God's eyes no matter what any man, woman or perverted church doctrine chooses to believe.** Exodus 21:22-25 specifically addresses any harm to a baby within a mother's womb caused on purpose or by accident. Real Christians understand that life is precious in the eyes of God and all who claim to belong to God. Psalm 139:14-18

22. **Those who support abortion condemn themselves in the eyes of God and Jesus by going directly against the teachings of Jesus concerning little children and by actions that are in support of evil.** Matthew 18:6, 10, 14; Matthew 19:14; John 14:15, 23; and, Mark 10:14.

23. **Homosexuality is evil and unacceptable in God's eyes no matter what any man, woman or perverted church doctrine chooses to believe.** Aside from the numerous verses in both the O.T. and N.T. that deal directly with this subject, the following scriptures should be considered in the hearts of those who claim to be God's people.

    a. "You shall not lie with a male as with a woman. It is an abomination." Leviticus 18:22

    b. "If a man lies with a man as he lies with a woman, both of them have committed an abomination. They shall surely be put to death. Their blood shall be upon them." Leviticus 20:13

    c. "But outside [of Heaven] are dogs and sorcerers and sexually immoral and murderers and idolaters, and whoever loves and practices a lie." Revelations 22:15

    d. "Who knowing the righteous judgment of God, that those who practice such things are worthy of death, not only do the same but approve of those who practice them." Rom 1:32

    e. Comment: From time immemorial, there have been those in the Church who taught that homosexuality and lesbianism are okay. Apostle Paul makes this clear in Romans 1-2. However, despite such perverted teachings, the word of God is plain on the matter

Copyright 2005 Edward G. Palmer, All Rights Reserved.

Book of Edward—Appendix C

Doctrinal Statement

for those who choose to accept and obey. Those who repent and change their ways in obedience to the will of God will be saved. Those who claim to belong to God and/or saved by Jesus Christ who actually practice homosexuality or lesbianism are cursed because they do not consider God's Holy Word and "take it to heart." See Malachi 2:2.

  i. "Therefore God also gave them up to uncleanness, in the lusts of their hearts, to dishonor their bodies among themselves, who exchanged the truth of God for the lie, and worshipped and served the creature rather than the CREATOR, who is blessed forever. Amen. For this reason God gave them up to vile passions. For even their women exchanged the natural use for what is against nature. Likewise also the men, leaving the natural use of the woman, burned in their lust for one another." Romans 1:24-27

  ii. "And in vain they worship ME, teaching as doctrines the commandments of men." Matthew 15:9 and Mark 7:7

24. **No righteousness, No salvation.** Matthew 5:20; Acts 10:34-35

25. **No obedience, No salvation.** Romans 6:16

  a. "No! For the Scriptures tell us that bread won't feed men's souls: *obedience* to every word of God is what we need." Matt. 4:4 LIV

  b. "Teach these new disciples to *obey* all the commands I have given you ..." Matthew 28:20

  c. Jesus says, "If you love me, *obey* me." John 14:15

  d. "You are my friends if you *do whatever I command* you." John 15:14

  e. "Do you not know that to whom you present yourselves slaves to obey, you are that one's slaves who you obey, whether of sin leading to death, or of *obedience* leading to *righteousness*." Romans 6:16

26. **Disciplining your body is the answer to your sin.** Matthew 5:29

Copyright 2005 Edward G. Palmer, All Rights Reserved.

Book of Edward—Appendix C

Doctrinal Statement

    a. "If your right eye causes you to sin, pluck it out and cast it from you; for it is more profitable for you that one of your members perish, than for your whole body to be cast into Hell." Matthew 5:29

        i. Contrary to what soft peddling preachers of today may say, Jesus actually does mean that it is better to be without a limb, eye, etc. if that is what it has to be to get your sin under control. The first response of your eye should be to look the other way. Stop looking at breasts, men, start looking at faces and into a woman's eyes. Stay away from porn shops, magazine racks and homosexual bars that tempt and draw you into sin.

        ii. Recognize that your imagination can win over your will power and that strong discipline is the answer. Limit your options to stop your sin. Stopping sin is exactly what Jesus is talking about when he said: "sin no more."

           1. Find a real believer to help you keep yourself honest with God.

           2. Get on a 12-step program for any offending member of your body.

        iii. It takes a willful act and a series of thought patterns and actions to commit sin. God says that *real* believers who have the Spirit of God can overcome sinful temptation. Those who walk the life will testify to God's truth.

           1. "You are of God … and have overcome them, because HE who is in you is greater than he who is in the world." 1 John 4:4

           2. "For whatever is born of God overcomes the world. And this is the victory that has overcome the world – our faith." 1 John 5:4

27. **WORKS are God's evidence of real faith and belief!**

    a. "HE will reward each according to his works." Matthew 16:27

    b. "Faith without works is dead." James 2:20

Doctrinal Statement

   c. "And behold, I am coming quickly, and MY reward is with ME, to give to everyone according to his work." Revelations 22:12

28. **HELL is real no matter what any man, woman or perverted church doctrine chooses to believe.** Matthew 10:28

    a. There are no second chances in Hell like some Christian sects preach. Their message is that even if you get to Hell, you will get a second chance down there. *Imagine* wreaking all the evil havoc you can while on planet earth in the flesh. You die and wind up in Hell. Jesus shows up to visit with you and says: "You see, I really do mean it. Now, don't you want to accept my offer of salvation and join me with God in Heaven?" You reply, "Jesus, you mean to tell me all this Heaven and Hell stuff is for real? Why, of course, I repent Jesus."

    b. One writer even asserts that Hitler is in Heaven and if you want to understand God, you have to understand why. If you believe that kind of "second chance" theology, you are already headed on your way towards Hell because you now make a mockery of all of God's Word concerning the godly and ungodly.

        i. "For the LORD knows the way of the righteous, but the way of the ungodly *shall* perish." Psalm 1:6

29. **God's new covenant holds you responsible for your own sins; and, God has not changed!**

    a. "Behold, the days are coming, says the LORD, when I will make a New Covenant." Jeremiah 31:31 "At that time ... each person will die for his own sin." Jer. 31:30 NCV

    b. "I will put MY law in their minds, and write it on their hearts, and I will be their God, and they shall be MY people." Jeremiah 31:33-34 Comment: God's New Covenant is about our own individual responsibility rather than the collective responsibility and punishment HE imposed earlier on Israel [Jer. 31: 27].

    c. A father is not responsible for the sins of his son and vice versa. Ezekiel 18:17-18 "I will judge everyone according to his ways.

Doctrinal Statement

Repent, and turn from all your transgressions, so that iniquity will not be your ruin." Ezekiel 18:30

d. "Cast away from you all the transgressions which you have committed, and get yourselves a new heart and a new spirit." Ezekiel 18:31

e. "I will give you a new heart and put a new spirit within you; I will take the heart of stone out of your flesh and give you a heart of flesh." Ezekiel 36:26

f. "I will put MY Spirit within you and cause you to walk in MY statutes, and you will keep MY judgments and do them." Ezekiel 36:27

g. "Therefore turn and live." Ezekiel 18:32

30. **There is only ONE God and not a trinity according to Jesus in his teachings about his God, the FATHER.**

    a. There is no scripture to support the doctrine of a triune God [three co-equal parts to God] in the Bible. Only a lack of spiritual discernment can explain the concept of a trinity. Many Christians simply do not know God because they have never listened to and obeyed the teachings of Jesus. They are ignorant and spiritually lazy people. Matthew 22:29 NCV

    b. "Hear, O Israel, the LORD our God, the LORD is ONE. And you shall love the LORD your God with all your heart, with all your soul, with all your mind, and with all your strength. This is the first commandment." These are Jesus' own words in Mark 12:29.

    c. "All Scripture is given by inspiration of God, and is profitable for doctrine, for reproof, for correction, for instruction in righteousness." 2 Timothy 3:16 God's word indicates that you need to understand both the Old Testament and the New Testament for any correct doctrine, as God has not changed. Therefore, you cannot ignore any scripture!

    d. "The Spirit of truth proceeds from the FATHER [God] and testifies of [Jesus]." John 15:26

Copyright 2005 Edward G. Palmer, All Rights Reserved.

Book of Edward—Appendix C

Doctrinal Statement

e. "These things say Jesus who has the *seven* Spirits of God" Rev 3:1. Note: Not only is there no support for a trinity, the doctrine also ignores six of *seven* (85.7%) of God's Spirits. And, Jesus makes it clear that the Holy Spirit, one of *seven*, comes from his God.

31. **The God of the Old Testament did not change in the New Testament.**

    a. "For I am the LORD [God], I do not change." Malachi 3:6

    b. "Have we not all ONE FATHER? Has not ONE God created us?" Malachi 2:10

    c. "A son honors his father, and a servant his master. If then I am the FATHER, where is MY honor? And if I am a MASTER, where is MY reverence? Says the LORD of hosts to you priests who despise MY name [by teaching false doctrine]." Malachi 1:6

    d. "Jesus Christ is the same yesterday, today and forever." Hebrews 13:8

    e. "A wife is responsible to her husband, her husband is responsible to Christ, and Christ is responsible to God." 1 Cor 11:3 LIV

    f. The N.T. cannot be read without understanding that God has not changed. You cannot take Paul out of context by trying to read his writings while ignoring the writings of Jesus, the other apostles, prophets and Moses. To take Paul and make his teachings negate or "trump" the words of Jesus makes such a person a Nicolaitan.

        i. "But this you have, that you hate the deeds of the Nicolaitans, which I also hate." Rev 2:6 [Jesus citing a good point about this church: hatred of lying Nicolaitans.]

        ii. "Thus you also have those who hold the doctrine of the Nicolaitans, which thing I hate." Rev 2:15 [Jesus condemning this church for having Nicolaitans inside of it.]

        iii. Note: The Nicolaitans perverted Paul's teachings and taught "moral looseness." Is this not a huge problem in the Christian Church today? Why? Ignorant people.

32. **Christ has not eliminated the Law.** Matthew 5:17-18

Copyright 2005 Edward G. Palmer, All Rights Reserved.

Book of Edward—Appendix C

Doctrinal Statement

- a. "Do not think that I came to destroy the Law or the Prophets. I did not come to destroy but to fulfill. For assuredly, I say to you, till Heaven and earth pass away, one jot or one tittle will by no means pass from the Law until all is fulfilled." Matthew 5:17-18

- b. Jesus says: "Woe to you ... for you pay tithes ... and have neglected the weightier matters of the law: justice and mercy and faith. These you ought to have done, without leaving the others [matters of the Law] undone. Matthew 23:23 "Obey the Law" Matthew 23:1-2 NCV.

- c. "Love does no harm ... therefore love is the fulfillment of the Law." Romans 13:10

- d. "Do you dishonor God through breaking the law?" Romans 2:23

- e. "For the lips of a priest should keep knowledge, and people should seek the Law from his mouth; for he is the messenger of the LORD of hosts. But you have departed from the way; you have caused many to stumble at the Law. You have corrupted the covenant ..." Malachi 2:7-8

- f. "You have wearied the LORD with your words; yet you say, 'in what way have we wearied HIM?' In that you say, 'everyone who does evil is good in the sight of the LORD, and HE delights in them,' or, 'where is the God of justice?' " Malachi 2:17

33. **Modern tithe teaching is an abomination unto God.** Tithing as taught in the Church ignores the worship aspects of the tithe law in Deut 14:22-29. Its main purpose today is to line the pockets of false preachers who pervert God's Word for personal gain and to lead people away from God by teaching friendship with the world.

34. **Forgiveness requires repentance.**

- a. "And if he sins against you seven times in a day, and seven times in a day returns to you, saying, I repent, you *shall* forgive him." Luke 17:4

- b. Comment: Is God going to forgive you if you do not repent? No. Will HE worry about you if you do not repent? I do not think so.

Doctrinal Statement

Will HE forgive you if you repent? Yes. Christians need to operate as God does. Forgiveness is not an option when someone does repent. We simply need to forgive as God forgives us.

    i. Forgiveness is not something that can be given out without repentance. The Church has long forgotten God's instructions and it is a major reason we have so many people sinning today. The majority of humanity no longer understands the role of repentance in the cessation of their sin. Has saying I'm sorry now lost its meaning?

    ii. "Therefore bear fruits worthy of repentance." Matthew 3:8

35. **A separated and holy people.**

    a. "And you shall be holy to ME [God], for I the LORD am holy, and have separated you from the peoples, that you should be MINE." Leviticus 20:26

    b. "But as HE who called you is holy, you also be holy in all your conduct, because it is written, "Be holy, for I am holy." 1 Peter 1:15

    c. "He who is unjust, let him be unjust still; he who is filthy, let him be filthy still; he who is righteous, let him be righteous still; he who is holy, let him be holy still." Rev 22:11

        i. An important aspect of God's love is HIS willingness to let you do your own thing on earth even if it is evil and results in your eternal damnation in Hell. The gift of free will that God gives us is never to be compromised by some kind of forced theology or a man made "guilt trip." God requires a willing and sincere heart from you. HE wants a love that is true from you. Would you have your earthly spouse be "forced" upon you or do you too also require a willing and sincere heart? A love that is true [willingly and not by force] from your spouse's heart?

36. **Christianity today has been reduced to mythology.** One standard message is: "You no longer have to obey God's commandments. Simply mouth Jesus as your Lord, give 10% of your gross income to the church and you now have it made in God's eyes.

Doctrinal Statement

All is forgiven, go and live your life however you want. Even if you wind up in Hell, a loving God will give you a second chance down there." Those who teach or believe these doctrines are servants of Satan and they will never see the kingdom of God. Matthew 6:24, etc.

37. **The current Christian mythology was prophesied about.**

   a. "For the time will come when men will not put up with sound doctrine. Instead, to suit their own desires, they will gather around them a great number of teachers to say what their itching ears want to hear. They will turn their ears away from truth and turn aside to myths." 2 Timothy 4:3-4 NIV

   b. "The coming of the lawless one will be in accordance with the work of Satan displayed in all kinds of counterfeit miracles, signs and wonders, and in every sort of evil that deceives those who are perishing. *They perish because they refused to love the truth* and so be saved. For this reason God sends them a powerful delusion so that they will believe the lie and so that all will be condemned who have not believed the truth but have delighted in wickedness." 2 Thessalonians 2:9-12 NIV

   c. "The prophecies in 2 Timothy 4:3-4 and 2 Thessalonians 2:9-12 are fulfilled. Today, mythology is routinely taught from the pulpits of many Christian churches instead of God's Holy Word and many people attending Christian churches have turned away from the truth. These people are headed toward Hell unaware of their lost souls." The Apostle Edward

38. **The Bible is not a book about Jesus. It is a book about God and how Jesus pointed the WAY back to his FATHER [his God].** A God so loving that HE would sacrifice HIS only begotten human Son [Jesus] to reconcile humankind with his need for justice. When you recognize that the trinity is a man made doctrine and mythology, you will start to understand God and HIS Son Jesus and what the "message" of the Holy Bible is really about.

   Since God has not changed …

Doctrinal Statement

    a. **The Message of the Holy Bible is the same in both the Old and New Testaments.** It is God's message of eternal salvation to those who repent and walk a godly life, a life of righteousness in God's eyes [according to God's word, not man-made doctrine].

    b. "If I had not come and spoken to them, they would have no sin, but now they have no excuse for their sin." Jesus in John 15:22

39. **God loves you and "has no pleasure in the death of one who dies. Therefore, turn [repent] and live."** Ezekiel 18:32 [In modern parlance, it means to "get a life" — a life <u>with</u> God!]

40. **Apostle Paul teaches salvation in Romans 10:9-10.** "[V9] If you confess with your mouth the Lord Jesus and believe in your heart that God has raised Jesus from the dead, you will be saved."

    a. [V10A]: "**For with the heart, one believes to righteousness.**" This means that your heart and everything inside of your being and spirit-soul now respects God and His commands. That you will now become a "slave to righteousness" putting aside all your prior sinful and evil ways. You will be obedient to God.

    b. [V10B]: "**And, with the mouth, confession is made to salvation.**" This means you now freely admit that God is real and you freely talk about how His Son has changed your life. Indeed, you are a <u>witness</u> to the world concerning how Jesus has brought you back to God.

Comment: Belief *unto* righteousness [righteous behavior in God's eyes] is ignored by the Church, which focuses on *mouthing* Jesus for your salvation. Verily I say unto you, that you can mouth Jesus until you're blue in the face on your way to Hell. If your heart has not been transformed *unto* righteous behavior and good works—you're spirit-soul is condemned and is not saved. If you study Matthew 7:21-23, you will have to ultimately conclude that real salvation transcends the ability to mouth Jesus as Lord. The Apostle Edward

Copyright 2005 Edward G. Palmer, All Rights Reserved.

Book of Edward—Appendix C

Appendix D
Jackie's Final Thoughts

The following are Jackie's final written thoughts that she penned prior to her death. Jackie wrote very little during our life except when I was in the U.S. Navy. I lament that I did not keep her letters like she kept mine. Who could know that within a mere 39 years of this earthly existence that I would long to read her penned love letters once again. The Apostle Edward

— Page 1 —

<u>Things I Love</u>
Snow geese flew right over my head yesterday. Last week an eagle was flying at the top of our trees.

— Page 2 —

I am not cancer. I have cancer. Hate the cancer, but remember you have to go through me to get to the cancer. I am a person with feelings, desires, etc.

Could I have caused the cancer? Maybe! Not on purpose. I have never ever wanted to hurt anyone. I believe there are a lot of things that can cause this enemy. I hope everyone can hate the cancer, not me. I love you all. I don't choose to leave everyone. I have spent my life loving and caring for everyone. Did I make mistakes? Sure—I'm not perfect. Forgive me, but always remember I tried to do my best.

Jackie's Final Thoughts

— Page 3 —

The saddest part for me is that I am hurting others in my life. I know what it feels like to lose a mother, father, child, brother and sister-in-law. I'm sure losing a spouse is even harder in some ways, but I don't really know since until you experience something, you never really know. One of the big lessons in life I've learned is that one. You never really know until you've been there.

It was so hard when I lost Glen. It left a place in me that could never be filled again. It was so hard when I lost my Dad. It was easy to let him go as he was so sick, but then there was that lonely time without him. I remember the good times before the cancer. I remembered the things he loved and the things he taught me. So many of the things I have loved he too loved— nature, children, people, etc. What a blessing he was in my life.

— Page 4 —

I think when my Mom died I was somewhat ready. She was kind of leaving us for years. I always kind of thought she lived passed her time. I think she felt she had to for us, especially Jim (Jackie's older brother). When she left I felt like an orphan. There was no other way to describe it. I also came to know her better. Who she was, what she felt, how she loved us, and more. I don't know how to explain. Maybe her spirit let me have the knowledge, which also gave me such peace.

When my brother left us I think I was somewhat ready even as I missed him terribly. He was such a blessing in my life. He also taught me how to die. He was ready I think when the time came (age 59). He felt he had a good life. (Jim had suffered for 25 years with heart problems and had more than one open-heart operation to extend his life. For 20 years or more Jackie and I felt that he lived on borrowed time, but God answered our prayers to keep him around. Thanks LORD!)

Copyright 2005 Edward G. Palmer, All Rights Reserved.

Book of Edward—Appendix D

Jackie's Final Thoughts

I put this writing aside as we got company so will now try to return to my thoughts. He [Jim] knew how to live each day, even though he knew death could come at any time on any given day. He loved life, his family and friends. He loved being with everyone and in his way started saying his good-byes in his own loving way. He left us with style. I hope I can do the same.

Yes my beloved, you did leave us with style. You were a class act all the way to getting your heavenly wings and I am very proud of you! You taught all of us that indeed there is no need to worry about this earthly death. Enjoy Heaven my love and I will see you at my own appointed time. The Apostle Edward

— Page 5 —

When we lost our dear Barb (Ed's sister) we also felt it was too soon (age 53). I think she was ready. She had fought a lot of (health) battles, but always lived close to angel like. She always gave so of all that she had. You always knew she loved you even if it wasn't always in words. She wasn't afraid to say the words either. I've been so lucky to have so many loving and good people in my life. I feel very blessed.

I've had so many people in my life that I truly felt a special connection to. I camped with some, danced with others, laughed with some and cried with some. I even remember delivering papers with one Uncle in my life. I would have to write a book to name all and to write each and every memory. A lot of wonderful times.

Jacqueline Lee (Bowers) Palmer died on June 3, 2003 at the age of 56 of pancreatic cancer 98 days after diagnosis.

Book of Edward

Appendix E
Ed's Goodbye Eulogy

How Do You Say Goodbye To Someone You've Loved 43 Years

On February 26, Jackie and I learned she had terminal pancreatic cancer. It had already metastasized onto her liver. The doctors said it was a stage four cancer with little hope. It was also the worse day of my 57 years of life. Jackie said several times during our 39-year marriage that she believed she wouldn't live past age 60. In contrast, I've always loved Genesis 6:3. That is where God says we could live to be 120. It still sounds good to me today despite many years of physical pain and now Jackie's death. You might imagine that as we approached our 50's together that I have encouraged Jackie to change her thinking on this very subject; but she never could.

Last Christmas Jackie told Paula and Patty that she thought it would be her last. I believe that God lets people know when their time on earth is fulfilled. Jackie always knew God's timing. I believe God told her His timing after we lost our first son Glen in 1965. God also told her that He would give her many more boys to replace the firstborn son we lost. We were both amazed over the years as God fulfilled His promise through Brian and seven grandsons. Each new boy was a gift from God along with His gift of three daughters and two granddaughters.

When Jackie and I learned of her diagnosis, I experienced two days of terrible chest pain followed by 7 days of lesser pain. It literally felt like my heart was being ripped out of my body. Pain ravaged my body over every thought of losing Jackie. She asked me several times if she should call 911 for me during the first 24 hours. I said no and told her, "It was just a broken heart over the thought of losing her."

Ed's Goodbye Eulogy

Jackie was a wonderful wife, mother, grandmother and friend. She was also a counselor to many who needed her help. Many of you loved her deeply like I did, especially our children, grandchildren and other family members. Some of you might also be experiencing a broken heart like me. If so, take comfort in the words of the Psalmist who writes.

> "The LORD is near to those who have a broken heart,
> And saves such as have a contrite spirit." [Psalm 34:18]

Indeed, it is God Almighty who stands near to our broken hearts. We are taught in Proverbs 3:5 to "Trust in the LORD with all your heart, and lean not on your own understanding." Why should we do this?

It is because there are actually two realities for our life. One is what we can pick up with our own human senses and the other is what God sees. Only God has the total picture of our life. That is why I confess to all of you, "My human understanding is totally useless in this time of our grieving."

It is only in God that I can find peace for my mind, spirit and body. I know that it is God who <u>now</u> holds Jackie in HIS loving and caring arms. My turn during her earthly life is over, so is yours. The prophet Isaiah records some important words on the subject of our peace. Isaiah 26:3 paraphrased reads:

> "God will keep you in perfect peace,
> When your mind is focused on HIM,
> Because you trust in HIM."

Jackie trusted in God. If you want peace during this time of grief, you will need to shift your focus from this limited earthly domain to God's unlimited heavenly domain. Peace for the loss of your grandmother, mother, friend, my wife and the loss of her love for all of us can only be found if we go to the place where Jackie found peace. What was the source of Jackie's peace?

Jackie found God's peace through the work of HIS only begotten Son Jesus Christ. Jesus gave her an understanding of God and of HIS Commandments.

Copyright 2005 Edward G. Palmer, All Rights Reserved.

Book of Edward—Appendix E

Ed's Goodbye Eulogy

Apostle John writes in 1 John 5:20, "And we know that the Son of God has come and has given us an understanding, that we may know HIM who is true; and we are in HIM who is true, in HIS Son Jesus Christ. This is the true God and eternal life."

Jackie came to know God because she accepted the gift of eternal salvation through the blood of Jesus Christ. She was a Christian all of the days that I knew her.

After the diagnosis, Jackie also told me that she believed her work on this earth was completed and it was time to go home. It was tough words that I didn't want to hear. However, it wasn't long before I realized that the physical pain I felt in my body was a result of a spiritual confirmation inside of me about Jackie's impending travel plans to Heaven. You see, God confirmed to my own spirit that it was indeed her time to go home.

The Psalmist writes in Psalm 31:14-15

> "But I trust in you, O LORD;
>   I say, 'YOU are my God.
>   My times are in your hands.'"

Jackie was comforted by these words of David on the face of a calendar she purchased after the diagnosis. She knew I would also be comforted by the words because she knew I loved God's Word. It seems like some confusion exists in Christianity today over God's healing power. Does God always heal his people? If so, why not heal Jackie? The quick answer is no, and the subject is too complicated to discuss in any meaningful way here today.

Jackie and I both knew that our times and life firmly rested in God's hands. Both of us are comfortable with that knowledge. We have always tried to teach our children and grandchildren to live each day well because we do not know if God will give us a tomorrow. God knows the number of our days and the plans HE has for our lives. Job says, "Does [God] not see my ways and count all my steps?" [Job 31:4] The words of the Psalmist that our life is in God's hands confront the idea that God heals everyone all the time; at

Ed's Goodbye Eulogy

least in the sense that we think of healing on this earth meaning a longer earthly life. Job confirms to us that it is God who is in control of life.

Despite all of our efforts at prayer and attempts at the use of alternative nutrition technologies, in the end, we were forced to yield to God's larger plan. I doubt if any of us can fully know or appreciate His larger plan for Jackie until we join her in eternity where there is no pain and no sorrow.

Jackie was raised in the Minneapolis community of Bryn Mawr by her mother Beverly and father Archie. She had a brother Jim and sister Candy. Her mom, dad and brother preceded her in death. Candy lives with her husband Al in New Hope.

Jackie attended the Bryn Mawr Presbyterian Church only a few blocks away from home. She was baptized as a baby and then confirmed in her faith around the age of 13. Jackie was an active Christian teen in her church where Pastor Searfoss taught her three basic messages of the Bible. Fear God, accept Jesus and be a good person. Just doing the right thing in life was an easy to accept message from God in those days. Today, however, these three Bible messages have been distorted and Christians are confused. In 1995, at the age of 49, Jackie expressed her faith in God once again through a water baptism by immersion at Lake Rebecca. Our grandson Christopher was baptized at the same time.

Jackie always liked wholesome activities that would edify and build up our character. She was the first to admonish me if I strayed from a godly life and character. She was also soft and tender. She was often a mitigating force against the harder edges of my personality. In many respects, God blended us together in our 39-year marriage. Jackie and I were one flesh.

I too was baptized as a baby and confirmed at the age of 13. However, it seems like nothing stuck to me in terms of spirituality until I reached the age of 32. That is the age when I found God. When I did find God, Jackie asked me what took me so long and said, "I've been waiting for you." It was a poignant moment for me that illustrated the depth of her simple faith in God. Jackie was more to me than a wife, friend and lover; she was also a helpmate sent by God Almighty to complete me so I could be all that God

Ed's Goodbye Eulogy

wanted me to be. Where I was weak, Jackie was strong and I always knew that she was God's gift to me.

It was Jackie who did the painting and remodeling projects at home. Of course, sometimes she just smashed a wall to get me going on a project she needed help with when I was reluctant to get started. That is what she did recently when the bathroom needed some work to get rid of mold.

To the extent we enjoyed a clean and lovely house, it was her handiwork, not mine. Jackie also liked to garden, sew, garage sale and finish furniture. She was also a veritable encyclopedia of help for all the gals and guys in the family who needed an answer. I remember many years that we had food on our table because she gardened. I also remember many years where her sewing clothed our children. Jackie and I knew we could choose different paths in life. We chose the path where she would maximize the family and home. She would stretch the dollars. I would try to get some and keep the roof over our heads. Jackie chose to be a homemaker. She wasn't just good at it; she was a natural caregiver who always looked out for the interests of the members of her family. Jackie was God's gift to our entire family and we will all miss her.

Jackie served on the board of Christian Education at one church we attended. She also served in the Jaycettes when I was in the Jaycees. We both tried to make our community a better place. Sometimes, her contribution was taking care of the home front, so I could contribute to some project or organization. I always knew my efforts were made possible because of her love for me. We viewed our lives as a team effort. To the extent I have accomplished anything in my life, it was because of her love for me. It was her love for me that always kept me going and she was the wind underneath my sails.

I was the dreamer and adventurer. Jackie was the pragmatist and she always tried to keep me grounded in the _full_ reality of life. I like to wander off into the unknown. I don't know why. For example: At Pike Lake in Wisconsin, I liked to venture into the lily patches with the boat. She would get scared and preferred a clear path on the lake that didn't present uncertainty. Same thing with those muddy roads being built that I liked to explore. "Don't go there, we might get stuck." When I jumped off of an entrepreneurial cliff, I

Ed's Goodbye Eulogy

was conscious that she was tethered to me with a bungee cord. And as her life drew near to an end, I could feel the cord that bonded our physical life together start to separate. The one flesh that God created with our marriage was dissolving as our marriage vow 'till death do us part' became fulfilled.

You should know that Jackie was reserved and did not like taking undo risks in life. She preferred to put her trust into solid and understandable things. That is why she put her trust in God. She couldn't see HIM, but she could feel HIM in her spirit. God wasn't an abstract idea for Jackie. HE was real.

I started chasing Jackie Bowers when she was just 13 years of age. I even asked her to marry me when I was 15 and she was 14. Can you believe that? What was I thinking? When we got married, she was only 17. Fifty-six less thirteen equals the forty-three years that I have loved Jackie. So, how do you say goodbye to someone you have loved forty-three years? That was the question my mind posed to me the day after we learned of her diagnosis. Today, I want you to know how I can say goodbye to the love of my life.

Our love story began with a simple kiss goodbye at a party Jackie had in the basement of her Bryn Mawr home. The year was 1960 and Jackie was then dating my best friend Joey. After Joey got his goodbye kiss, I asked for one and guess what? She gave me one. It was a kiss that would alter our lives and it is still alive in my memory. I immediately told my friend that if he ever left her that I would be chasing after her. He did drop the ball.

It was a common thing for 18 year olds to go out into the world and make a life for themselves. Maturity levels were substantially higher in those days. I joined the Navy at age 17 and gave Jackie the ultimatum to marry me at age 18 or I would move on with my life. After she graduated in 1964, we got married. I think my Navy uniform carried the day for me. At least that is what she always claimed. She said something about getting taken in by a sailor's uniform. Jackie didn't have to marry me. Joey came chasing after her again and even after we were married she had several other propositions to leave me. She was loved that much at just age 17.

It was on Tuesday, May 13th that Jackie took a turn for the worse. I thought she might have had a stroke, so we took her to the emergency room. The

Ed's Goodbye Eulogy

pain meds were not doing the job and probably causing the severe side affects that were present. The solution was to change pain medication. Tuesday and into Wednesday were really rough. I honestly did not know if she would make it. The Hospice crew was in a state of disbelief over her health. Jackie always had a unique way of her own, even with this illness.

Of course, our answer to the crisis was prayer because we trust in the same God. I don't remember having much more than a few hours sleep when Jackie woke up at 3 am on Thursday morning May 15th. She was ready to go after having "rested" for two days. She started all kinds of activities even though almost blind. She could see and feel her way around enough to want to get some things done. I asked her at 3:30 am, "Do you know what time it is?" Like she really cared with all that rest. By 5:30 am, I called Candy for help. I know it was that time because Candy reminded me. By the time Candy arrived at 6:30 am, I was thinking, "Jackie is going to drive me nuts again." Such was the nature of my emotions.

Later in the day I had a conversation with God and I had to start laughing at the sheer dichotomy of my emotions. I couldn't stop crying on Tuesday and Wednesday. Now, on Thursday it seemed like she would drive me nuts. It wasn't the first time I had those emotions. When you decide to spend your life with someone, those emotions will occur. What is it that bridges the gap between your tears at the thought of loss and your angst at going nuts? It is love and Proverbs 10:12 teaches us that, "Hatred stirs up strife, but love covers all sins." When you choose to love someone, you recognize that they are not perfect; but you choose to love them anyway. Both Jackie and I learned to master the art of God's love, especially the aspect of forgiveness.

I can tell you, that in the 43 years I have loved Jackie—she has chosen to forgive my sins countless times. Likewise, I have chosen to forgive her sins countless times. Indeed, the very nature of a true love story rests in this forgiveness attribute of God, which is given freely to all who truly believe.

Jesus taught Jackie in Matthew 10:28, "And do not fear those who kill the body but cannot kill the soul. But rather fear HIM who is able to destroy both soul and body in Hell."

Copyright 2005 Edward G. Palmer, All Rights Reserved.

Ed's Goodbye Eulogy

Jackie chose to believe in a God who offered her an eternal life that transcended her limited earthly existence. Jesus taught Jackie in John 14:2, "In my FATHER'S house are many mansions; if it were not so, I would have told you. I go to prepare a place for you."

Jesus taught Jackie in John 14:3-4, "And if I go and prepare a place for you, I will come again and receive you to myself; that where I am, there you may be also. And where I go you know, and the way you know."

Jesus also taught Jackie in John 13:36, "Where I am going ... you <u>shall</u> follow me." Jackie knew that Jesus went back to sit at the right hand of God Almighty, our FATHER, in Heaven. She believed in God who is the FATHER and she believed in the FATHER'S resurrection unto eternal life of Jesus Christ, God's Son who came to us in a human body of flesh and blood. Because of her understanding, she accepted the words of Jesus and knew her way home.

The Prophet Jeremiah [31:34] records the words of God which say, "No more shall every man teach his neighbor, and every man his brother, saying, 'Know the LORD,' for they all shall know ME, from the least of them to the greatest of them, says the LORD. For I will forgive their iniquity, and their sin I will remember no more."

Jeremiah records God's gift of love and forgiveness for all of us to learn. To the extent Jackie and I had an endless love for one another, it is only because we reflected God's love back to each other. "For I will forgive Ed or Jackie's iniquity, and their sin I will remember no more." God's love is at the heart of every enduring love affair. That was the secret of our long marriage.

The nature of God's love for all of us has some imprints. We cannot escape what God has imprinted on our minds and hearts. We cannot escape what God has imprinted on all of HIS creation. These imprints are a witness to all human flesh and they cannot be denied. All of us must acknowledge that God does exist at some point. Sooner, rather than later, we need to choose to be the good person that God expects us to be. Jackie understood these basic Bible teachings and she took them to heart and obeyed God.

Copyright 2005 Edward G. Palmer, All Rights Reserved.

Book of Edward—Appendix E

Ed's Goodbye Eulogy

"For God so loved the world that HE gave HIS only human begotten Son, that whoever believes in HIM should not perish but have everlasting life." If you want to understand John 3:16, you only have to understand the love that Jackie was able to reflect into this world. In the simplest terms, Jackie was like Jesus. She was an instrument of God used to reflect HIS love into our lives. The love she reflected from God has many seeds that will operate throughout our lives for generations to come. That is the legacy of her life.

Jesus said in John 14:28, "If you loved me, you would rejoice because I said, 'I am going to the FATHER,' for my FATHER is greater than I." Indeed, Jackie has now gone to the same place and we should all rejoice. This doesn't happen fast, because sorrow comes first. Sirach 38:16-21 teaches:

> My child let your tears fall for the dead,
>   And as one in great pain begin the lament.
> Lay out the body with due ceremony,
>   And do not neglect the burial.
> Let your weeping be bitter and your wailing fervent;
>   Make your mourning worthy of the departed,
> For one day, or two, to avoid criticism;
>   Then be comforted for your grief.
> For grief may result in death,
>   And a sorrowful heart saps one's strength.
> When a person is taken away, sorrow is over;
>   But the life of the poor weighs down the heart.
> Do not give your heart to grief;
>   Drive it away, and remember your own end.
> Do not forget, there is no coming back;
>   You do the dead no good, and you injure yourself."

If you believe in the God that Jackie believed in, you will understand that there is a time to mourn and a time to rejoice. I will focus on the good times I had with Jackie. I will remember her love and the instructions from God not to weigh my heart down with grief. Jackie has gone to a great place of joy. Likewise, I ask all my children, grandchildren, family and all who loved Jackie to remember her with the fullness of your joy. Do not be sad

Copyright 2005 Edward G. Palmer, All Rights Reserved.

Book of Edward—Appendix E

Ed's Goodbye Eulogy

for long because it would make Jackie sad. Hers was a specialty aimed at making our hearts glad. Let us live up to the joy she sought for our lives.

All of us can celebrate the joys of her life and the lovely memories Jackie gave to us. Memories. Wow. I have 43 years of them and I will cherish every one. Yet I know that Jackie would want me to continue on with my own life. God knows what the next phase will be. I don't. I can only yield to HIS direction and take comfort in the fact that Jackie is now watching to see if I too will be faithful to our God even unto my own death.

This life is but a speck of dust in all of eternity. I know it in the core of my soul that I will see Jackie very soon. In the blink of an eye from our FATHER in Heaven, I will see her again in the glory of her eternal life with Jesus.

I can say goodbye to Jackie after loving her for 43 years because I know where Jackie has gone. Indeed, she is now in an eternal place of joy, peace and understanding where there is no more pain and sorrow. She is now surrounded by love in its purest form and love from those in her family that preceded her. Jackie now sees the big picture of her life and ours. I imagine that Baby Glen is updating her on family events and showing her the ropes.

Enoch writes, "For in [Jesus] name they are saved, and according to his good pleasure hath it been in regard to their life." [48:7]. He also writes, "And the righteous shall be victorious in the name of the LORD of Spirits: And HE will cause the others to witness this that they may repent and forgo the works of their hands" [50:2]. Jackie's life was a witness for God to us.

It is written in Enoch 81:4, "Blessed is the man [or woman] who dies in righteousness and goodness, concerning whom there is no book of unrighteousness written, and against whom no day of judgment shall be found." God doesn't care how rotten your life has already been. It only matters what your choice is now, before your death. It is never too late to experience the joy of knowing what Jackie knew about God's salvation.

If you do not have the peace of eternal life that Jackie had, please take time to talk to Chaplain Dale Swan or myself. We will help you understand what Jackie knew about life after death.

Copyright 2005 Edward G. Palmer, All Rights Reserved.

Book of Edward—Appendix E

Ed's Goodbye Eulogy

When Jackie and I lost our first son Glen back in 1965, it took God and time to heal our broken hearts. The following song by the Christian group Newsong, titled "God and Time," tells the story of how our hearts got over our grief and got healed.

Reverend Edward G. Palmer
Husband and Friend

The Apostle Edward delivered the above eulogy on June 7, 2003.

Appendix F
Cancer Killing Protocols

"The following twelve 'Cancer Killing Protocols' are the alternative nutritional strategies that God guided my spirit to for Jackie's cancer. She was unable to benefit from the protocols due to the metastasized nature of her cancer and our inability to expediently implement the cures. Cost was a critical factor in our case. To fully use all thirty strategies God guided me to would require the consumption of 100 or more pills per day and a fulltime effort. It also requires a personal assistant and coach to help deal with the scheduled intake of such a massive quantity of nutrients, which is an hourly endeavor. It is unlikely that someone suffering from pancreatic cancer can succeed on his or her own without fulltime family help. Further details on God's cancer killing protocols can be found on my ministry's web site at http://www.informcentral.org. For God's Glory!" The Apostle Edward

TWELVE CANCER KILLING PROTOCOLS

1. Vitamin B17 therapy as outlined by Oasis of Hope Hospital protocol.
2. Budwig Diet using organic cottage cheese with flaxseed oil.
3. Eliminate all process foods; if God didn't make it, don't eat it.
4. Eliminate all forms of sugar intake; cancer feeds on sugar.
5. Trace minerals & super greens to improve body's Ph level.
6. Oxygen therapy to improve body's Ph level.
7. Consume a quality multi-vitamin and mineral nutrient product.
8. Heat therapy to bake cancer cells into over metabolizing themselves.
9. MGN-3 to enhance body's natural killer cells.
10. L-Lysine with Vitamin C to shrink tumors and prevent metastasis.
11. Ambrotose to improve cell-cell health communications.
12. Exercise and massage to maintain lymph circulatory system cleansing.

Cancer Killing Protocols

Disclaimer: This information is not intended to offer medical or legal advice and is only offered for informational purposes. Use at your own risk. Any cancer patient, who does not accept personal responsibility for his or her own cure will not find one easily. And, if your solution is to rely upon just medical doctors, you may be disappointed and broke before you are cured.

> **"Now a woman, having a flow of blood for twelve years, who had spent all her livelihood on physicians and could not be healed by any, came from behind and touched the border of his garment. And immediately her flow of blood stopped." Luke 8:43-44**

On my bookshelf is a two-inch thick three ring binder of cancer cure information. I have literally poured over hundreds and thousands of pages on the subject. The binder represents distilled critical information and this appendix represents the top twelve strategies that I would use. If you only deploy a few, use them in the order listed, as this is my opinion on what my best tactics would be. If you take the time to search the Internet, you will find some incredible approaches. The woman with the flow of blood spent twelve years and went broke spending her money on doctors. In a touch of Jesus' garment, she was cured instantly.

In my studies, I have come to appreciate how God has also created our bodies with curative capabilities. All we have to do in most cases is feed the body the nutrients it needs to affect its own cures. From a cellular and even a DNA perspective, the body, if treated respectfully can cure itself and live to a long life. In contrast, a person who abuses his or her body can do the body in at an early age. I have seen several family members waste away needlessly at an early age because of bad health habits. Don't expect any cures to work if you can't stop smoking or alcohol intake. The cures shown here require discipline to work. Discipline starts by eliminating all personal abusive body habits. Having said that, do everything in your power to touch God with HIS Spirit. That too is a part of your cure. I believe the alternative approaches are incompatible with many traditional medical protocols so the biggest and first choice is whether to go with your doctor's plan or your own plan and your body's instincts. Or, create a compatible combination plan.

Copyright 2005 Edward G. Palmer, All Rights Reserved.

Book of Edward—Appendix F

Cancer Killing Protocols

Protocol Notes

1. **Vitamin B17**

    a. <u>Apricots Seeds</u>

    i. My first personal cancer fighting choice.
    ii. Kills cancer cells via targeted action.
    iii. Apricot seeds have a high concentration of B17.
    iv. Apricot seeds are relatively cheap online.
    v. Obtain further information at www.cancure.org
    vi. Obtain further information at www.1cure4cancer.com
    vii. Build tolerance up to 12-20 Apricot seeds per day.
    viii. Do not exceed 6 seeds per hour or 30 per day.
    ix. One seed per 10 pounds of body weight per day is considered safe. The above dosage was for 100-pound woman and was therapeutic in design.
    x. Protocols found in Dr. G. Edward Griffin's *"World Without Cancer"* book and video.
    xi. Most fruit seeds contain B17. Cherries, peaches, etc.
    xii. Crunch Apple seeds when eating to obtain its B17 or else the seeds will pass through intestine without nutrient use.

    b. <u>Laetrile Pill Form</u>

    i. Laetrile is drug form of B17 found in fruit seeds.
    ii. Oasis of Hope Hospital protocol found online.
    iii. Kills cancer cells via targeted action.
    iv. Build up to 3 grams per day and maintain for 30 days minimum. Available in 100 and 500 mg tablets.
    v. Also available in Injectable form for use with IV's.
    vi. Supervised protocol available in Mexican Hospital.
    vii. B17 can be taken rectally if not tolerated in stomach.
    viii. Both pills and seeds can be ground up and put into larger gelatin capsules and used rectally.

2. **Budwig Diet**

    a. Mix 1 cup of organic cottage cheese 1-2% fat with 3 tablespoons of organic liquid flaxseed oil. Eat daily.

Cancer Killing Protocols

  b. Obtain flaxseed oil from refrigerated section of food store only.
  c. Fruit can be mixed in to make it more palatable.
  d. Oxygenates body by supplying it with an abundance of free electrons, which are found in the flaxseed oil.
  e. The cottage cheese makes the flaxseed oil water-soluble so the body more easily absorbs the free electrons.
  f. Developed in Europe by Dr. Johanna Budwig and used for over four decades as a diet cure for degenerate metabolic diseases.
  g. Had an observable impact on Jackie's health, but she would not maintain the protocol, which was tough for her to consume.
  h. Keep doing it until cured.
  i. My second best curative choice.

3. **Process foods**
  a. Like bad health habits, process foods are part of the body's problem and you need to cease all such intake due to the chemical cocktails contained in process foods.
    i. Lunch meats, prepackaged foods, etc.
  b. Feeds cancer cell growth.
  c. Burdens liver functions with toxin removal.
  d. Get and eat food in a raw state. Don't cook out the nutrients.
  e. Dietary schedules of cancer patients need family assistance.

4. **Sugars**
  a. Cancer is a fermentation process that thrives on all forms of artificial sugar. Therefore, eliminate these sugars in the diet, which feed the fermentation process.
  b. It is possible to "starve" cancer cells, which require a lot of fermentation nutrients to grow. Normal body cells are unaffected by processed sugar deprivation.
  c. Processed sugar feeds cancer cell growth through an anaerobic [oxygen deprived] process.
  d. Sugars cause an acidic body state with low Ph levels of 4-6.

5. **Ph level**
  a. Cancer cannot flourish in a body with a high alkaline Ph state.
  b. The body should be tested for its Ph level.

Copyright 2005 Edward G. Palmer, All Rights Reserved.

Book of Edward—Appendix F

Cancer Killing Protocols

  c. Simple saliva strips can test the body's Ph level.
  d. Cancer patients have an acidic body state that feeds disease.
  e. "Greens" can move the body to the alkaline Ph state.
  f. Both Ph strips and a variety of "greens" can be found online.

6. **Oxygen**
    a. Liquid oxygen is available to help stabilize and move the body's Ph level to an alkaline state.
    b. Jackie used a product called "Oxy-Heal" which was easy to use.
    c. Kills cancer cells by oxygenating the body.
    d. Spray 7-8 squirts into mouth 3 times a day.
    e. Hold in mouth 30 seconds before swallowing.
    f. Cancer cells cannot stand oxygen.

7. **Vitamins**
    a. A good multivitamin-mineral package is essential for the body.
    b. After studying several, I chose the "Daily Advantage."
    c. I chose this package due to its "super greens" content.
    d. Dr. David Williams produces the Daily Advantage program.
    e. Take 2 packets of capsules daily with food.
    f. Each packet contains six pills.

8. **Heat**
    a. Cancer cells cannot stand higher body temperatures.
    b. Use heat packs and hot tubs to force cancer cells to work hard.
    c. Cancer cells can metabolize themselves to death via heat.

9. **MGN-3**
    a. Triples body's natural killer cell activity.
    b. Boosts immune system to enhance killer cell activity.
    c. Proven as an effective cancer therapy and recommended by two alternative cure books.
    d. Take 1 capsule 3 times daily.

10. **L-Lysine**
    a. Strengthens body's collagen fibers, which inhibits the metastasis process and prevents cancer spreading easily.
    b. Take ten 1,000 mg capsules daily.

Cancer Killing Protocols

    c. Take with same level of Vitamin C.
    d. Dr. Matthias Rath developed protocol.
    e. Online study available for download on efficacy.

11. **Ambrotose**
    a. Kills cancer cells by improving cell-cell communications.
    b. Take 1 capsule 3 times daily.
    c. Plant Saccharides are a newly developed glyconutritional that improves the immune system ability to kill off unwanted cells.
    d. Further information is available at www.mannatech.com.

12. **Exercise**
    a. The second major circulation system in the body is the lymph system, which moves waste in the body to the liver for removal.
    b. Exercise helps the lymph system function.
    c. Massage therapy also helps the lymph system function.
    d. Unlike the circulation system, which has "pipes" — the lymph system is the fluid that surrounds all cells. If the body is tied in knots [tense], it may not function to eliminate waste as it was designed.

Some Other Strategies

The above twelve strategies are the tactics that I would use to cure cancer in my own body. Of course, I would also use intense prayer and getting into God's presence. I assumed that a lot of water intake is also present for the above items. When it came to Jackie's pancreatic cancer, these other items were also found useful albeit we never got into the full protocols of these alternative-healing strategies. Personally, I would use as many as practical from a budget and swallowing perspective. Since I already am accustomed to swallowing a large number of nutraceuticals, I would have an easier time than Jackie.

13. **Water**
    a. Improves immune system by flushing body.
    b. Drink 8 glasses of water daily as a minimum intake.
    c. Flushes toxins out of body.

Copyright 2005 Edward G. Palmer, All Rights Reserved.

Book of Edward—Appendix F

Cancer Killing Protocols

14. **Pancreatic Enzymes**
    d. Pancreatic enzymes will help body.
    e. Helps reduce pain.
    f. Helps food get digested.
    g. Available from Doctor's prescription.
    h. Take 1 capsule with each meal to help digest foods.
    i. Standard medical protocol for pancreatic problems.
    j. We now lack a lot of enzymes that we used to get in food.

15. **Megazyme Forte**
    a. Enhances efficacy of B17.
    b. A good enzyme formulation more comprehensive.
    c. Available to purchase online.
    d. Take 3 capsules three times daily between meals.
    e. Dr. Francisco Contreras' Oasis of Hope protocol.

16. **Vitamin B15**
    a. Oxygenates body, improving efficacy of B17.
    b. Take one capsule after each meal.
    c. Available like most nutrients for purchase online.
    d. Dr. Francisco Contreras' Oasis of Hope protocol.

17. **A-E Emulsified**
    a. Enhances body's immune system.
    b. Liquid form of Vitamins A and E that allows for therapeutic doses to take place [of Vitamin A] beyond what pills allow.
    c. Oasis of Hope protocol calls for 225,000 IU units of "A" daily.
    d. This liquid form allows this protocol to take place.

18. **Selenium**
    a. Enhances body's immune system.
    b. Take three 200-mcg tablets daily to augment Daily Advantage.
    c. 800-mcg daily needed to fight cancer.

19. **Vitamin C**
    a. Take in conjunction with L-Lysine in comparable amount.
    b. Liquid Vitamin C available in bio available form eases intake.
    c. Some protocols call for up to 25,000 mg daily intake.

Cancer Killing Protocols

20. **Coral Calcium**
    a. Enhances body's immune system.
    b. Take 1-500 mg tablet 3 times a day.

21. **Probiotic**
    a. Lactobacillus Acidolphus is good bacteria that the intestine needs to function properly.
    b. Take two capsules daily to enhance digestive track.
    c. Standard medical protocol.

22. **Melatonin**
    a. Improves sleep and enhances immune system.
    b. Take 6 mg one hour prior to going to sleep.
    c. Range of intake is 3-12 mg.
    d. Mother hormone that body produces but is reduced after age 50.

23. **Coenzyme Q-10**
    a. Enhances body's immune system.
    b. Take 2-200mg softgels to augment Daily Advantage.
    c. Improves heart and cell functions.

24. **Colostrum**
    a. Enhances body's immune system.
    b. Take 1-650 mg tablet daily.
    c. Cited as effective in several online therapy recommendations.
    d. No specific mg intake cited in protocols.

25. **Vitamin B12**
    a. Take 1,000-2,000 mcg daily.
    b. Enhances mental faculties and memory functions.
    c. Dr. Julian Whitaker anti-cancer program specified 1,000 mcg.
    d. Recommended by Cancer Treatment Centers of America.

26. **Milk Thistle**
    a. Enhances body's immune system.
    b. Take 1-175 mg capsule daily.
    c. No specific mg cited as a protocol.

Copyright 2005 Edward G. Palmer, All Rights Reserved.

Book of Edward—Appendix F

Cancer Killing Protocols

27. **Dong Quai**
    a. Enhances body's immune system.
    b. Take 1-530 mg capsule daily.
    c. No specific mg cited as a protocol.

28. **Olive Leaf Extract**
    a. Natural Antimicrobial agent
    b. Take two capsules daily.
    c. Kills microbes inside the body.
    d. Functions as an antibiotic tonic to the body.

29. **Diet**
    a. Multiple sites list various foods to avoid or consume.
    b. Food intake feeds or starves cancer cells.
    c. Proper diet can really enhance survivability.
    d. Cancer patient cannot be expected to do all this alone.

30. **Colon Cleansing**
    a. Regular colon cleansing can enhance healing.
    b. An estimated 7-21 pounds of human waste attaches itself to walls of large colon.
    c. Disease breeds within the waste attached to the colon walls.
    d. Cleansing colon eliminates this waste and disease breeding.
    e. A clean colon is allows the liver to improve its efficiency in the removal of toxins.
    f. Cleanse with coffee animas daily. Up to 4 a day recommended by some protocols.
    g. Alternatively, use a colon-cleansing product and follow the instructions.

A word on expectations is due. I experienced some sickness, which involved stomach problems. I was unable to get or keep much of anything down. In serious cancers, you may have an uphill battle just trying to get anything down. You can offset pills by incorporating them into smoothies or other liquids. Also, don't overlook the rectal intake of B17 and other nutrients if the stomach cannot take it. My prayer is that this information will give you a strong starting point. Blessings. The Apostle Edward

Copyright 2005 Edward G. Palmer, All Rights Reserved.

Book of Edward—Appendix F

Book of Edward

Appendix G
Illustrations, Tables & Lists

238 Illustrations, Tables & Lists

Volume I

No.	Title/Description	Page
1	Priorities	13
2	God's communications plan	22
3	B.I.B.L.E.	23
4	People who are excluded from Heaven	38
5	Walking with God	43
6	Daily repentance prayer	57
7	Specific repentance prayer	57
8	Practice & do not practice checklist	88
9	Good works v. minimum righteousness standard	106
10	Walking with God v. min righteousness standard	108
11	Scripture citations connect the dots	117
12	Leap of faith required for dots to connect	118
13	Ninety-six apostles identified	123
14	Descriptions of apostle task or mission	124
15	Basic choice diagram for God or Satan	139
16	Force of righteousness or sin choice	140
17	A choice from the heart for God	144
18	A pattern of choices for God	145
19	A choice from the heart for Satan	145
20	A pattern of choices for Satan	146
21	The two turfs of life defined	147
22	Relative strength in the two turfs of life	148
23	The wide path leads to destruction	151
24	The narrow path leads to eternal life	153

Illustrations, Tables & Lists

25	Non-perfect narrow walk pattern	154
26	Backslider pattern	156
27	True repentance pattern	157
28	We can make bold choices from the heart	159
29	Real conviction pattern	160
30	The wide path leads to destruction #2	161
31	God & Satan's turf have four zones	164
32	Seven spiritual choices in life	168

Volume II

33	Hermeneutic principles of biblical interpretation	180
34	Two percent off at start misses target	182
35	Two percent off target is subtle	183
36	Errant teachings are cumulatively off course	184
37	The Holy Bible is 98% exoteric!	189
38	God's breath gives us understanding!	200
39	Seven keys to really understanding God's Word	203
40	Taking a circuitous trip with God	208
41	Two millennial old dig	215
42	Rationalization v. truth	222
43	Trinity symbol of Trinity Episcopal Church	252
44	New King James Bible trinity symbol	253
45	Interlocking fishes	254
46	Interlocking 6's?	254
47	Trinity citations rated (Hagee's)	258
48	Lost books referenced in Bible	264
49	Leap of faith required for dots to connect #2	275
50	Trinity citation summary (Hagee)	276
51	Trinity citation frequency analysis	277
52	Bibles v. commas in Luke 23:43	284
53	Bibles v. one in Mark 10:18	294
54	God has seven Spirits, not one!	301
55	Attributes of Jesus v. attributes of God	302
56	Summary of God's seven Spirits	304
57	Scripture teaches Christians	305
58	Scripture teachings continued	306

Copyright 2005 Edward G. Palmer, All Rights Reserved.

Book of Edward—Appendix G

Illustrations, Tables & Lists

59	One-way	324
60	Life as a stack of 100 deeds	327
61	A generally good person	329
62	A generally evil person	330
63	On balance, I am a good person	330
64	God's view, life as a stack of deeds	331
65	Spirit of Christ moves us from sin to righteousness	333
66	Draw close to God & HE draws close to you!	364
67	God's presence	365
68	God of Abraham	366
69	Circle of God, God's Spirit & Jesus	373
70	Seven abominations to God Almighty!	374
71	God's eternal character & sovereignty	380
72	Push "1" to turn God on	383
73	King David's walk, adultery & murder	402
74	Salvation line forms at Jesus' right side	404
75	Christianity has the wrong focus!	407
76	Whoever believes in Jesus	408
77	Salvation outside of Christ	410
78	Salvation truth table — 25 Bible facts	414
79	Your whole being is "spirit, soul & body!"	419
80	Death occurs when our spirit-soul leaves our body	421
81	Soul starting to obey Spirit's direction	424
82	Walking in the spirit	425
83	Walking in the flesh	425
84	What happens to "whole-being" at death!	426
85	Your essence manifested to humanity	427
86	God's communications channel	430
87	Satan's communications channel	431
88	No neutral [soul] position	432
89	The truth about Jesus	461
90	Phase 1: God starts with a direct relationship	462
91	Phase 2: sin alters spiritual influence	464
92	Phase 3: Satan wins Man's Souls	465
93	Phase 4: God sends sacrifice of Christ	467
94	Phase 5: God sends Spirit of truth	469
95	Strength of influence on man	470

Copyright 2005 Edward G. Palmer, All Rights Reserved.

Illustrations, Tables & Lists

96	Strength of influence characteristics	471
97	Characteristics of the gift of Jesus	488

Volume III

98	Peace in this earthly journey	497
99	Attributes of healing	511
100	Don't let bad habits evolve into death	518
101	List of healing verses for your own prayers	519
102	The spirit-soul life as God designed	522
103	The spirit-soul life In Satan's world	523
104	You in Satan's world with Holy Spirit	524
105	Prayer of faith formula	536
106	Minnesota Council of Churches backs Gays	550
107	Hoogenboom sex scandal article	558
108	Type of Protestant Church v. drawing close to God	560
109	Commitment to Word v. drawing close to God	561
110	Nine facts about religious teachers from Jesus	563
111	Seven questions to see if your Church is righteous	564
112	Six question to see if your Church serves God	565
113	Use of emotion in service v. drawing close to God	574
114	Fifteen spiritual warnings!	580
115	Type of Protestant Church v. drawing close to God #2	584
116	Type of Protestant Church v. drawing close to God #3	585
117	Seven signs of a satanic church	586
118	Heart knowledge of God v. drawing close to God	587
119	How a confused church supported evil!	594
120	How community players supported evil!	596
121	You only see isolated events	601
122	But, the swindler sees linear events	601
123	Exposed con reveals connections	602
124	Eight seemingly isolated Solid Rock events	602
125	Diary note recording meeting event	604
126	False corporate resolution sent to AFCM	611
127	Notice of mortgage foreclosure sale	612
128	Tithing instructions from God & His Son!	620
129	Three year tithe law instructions	622

Copyright 2005 Edward G. Palmer, All Rights Reserved.

Book of Edward—Appendix G

Illustrations, Tables & Lists

130	Tithe & lawlessness connection	623
131	Four distinctions in God's instructions	627
132	Five distinctions in book of Deuteronomy	627
133	Tithing is living under the ceremonial laws	628
134	Five characteristics of true believers	630
135	Four commands important to God & His Son	635
136	Righteousness (doing what's right)	638
137	Communication with God before Christ	646
138	Christ created a new communications model	647
139	Sabbath instructions	650
140	Signs of lawlessness and faith	658
141	The "Law" to those "in Christ"	659
142	Five facts about those who tithed in the Bible	668
143	Nine attributes of love	683
144	Abortions in the U.S.	688
145	Seven political facts about abortions	688
146	Communications model from mind to heart	695
147	Signers of U.S. Constitution—39	699
148	Fetal development facts from an abortion clinic	705
149	Four baby facts	709
150	Would you abort quiz	709
151	Ultrasound facts about babies	710
152	Doctor holds tiny baby!	716
153	Baby in womb holds doctor's finger	717
154	Only God knows your future descendants	718
155	From Abraham to Jesus there are 41 generations	723
156	Get the blood-life-soul picture?	732
157	Picture of 6-week old 1/2 inch 1/2 ounce fetus	737
158	Want mercy? Then proclaim mercy!	740
159	God's character & theology consistent with it	744
160	God's character in context of what He loves & hates	744
161	If you can't hate, you don't know God!	745
162	Four attributes of reason that control sin	752
163	Reason is heart's guard — communications model	754
164	Three primary thought sources "with God"	758
165	Two primary thought sources "without God"	759
166	Thoughts, then actions, and then emotions!	761

Copyright 2005 Edward G. Palmer, All Rights Reserved.

Book of Edward—Appendix G

Illustrations, Tables & Lists

167	Two thought self-contained action/sin model	763
168	Three levels of sexual sin	766
169	Bibles v. lewdness, Judges 20:6 KJV example	769
170	Bibles v. lasciviousness, Jude 1:4 KJV example	770
171	Bibles v. licentious, 2 Timothy 3:3 NAB example	770
172	Summary of God's nakedness rules!	784
173	Three ways to exceed minimum righteousness rule	790
174	Blue chip corporations profit from porn industry	803
175	Seven attributes of lasciviousness	807
176	Sexually immoral practices	842
177	Thirty Bible statements about homosexuals	850
178	Top ten Gay cities v. percent of city population	851
179	Signers of U.S. Constitution #2	853
180	For teens, sex & drugs go together	855
181	Love and sex are both choices of the heart!	866
182	Nine facts about the choice of love, marriage and sex	875
183	Sex falls into God's and Satan's zones	885
184	Sexual activity v. mortal sin table	887
185	Lewd, lascivious, licentious examples	889
186	Eight explanations God will ask you for	890
187	Fourteen things Democrats support	902
188	Eight things Democrats and Republicans support	903
189	Gallup's poll shows Nation morally divided	908
190	Religion & Ethics: how Christians voted	909
191	Biblical morality formula	912
192	Six ways Gay marriage impacts heterosexual marriage	913
193	Fourteen consequences of Church-State separation	918
194	God's moral values table I	919
195	God's moral values table II	921
196	Control of House & majority leader	932
197	Control of Senate & majority leader	933
198	Control of U.S. Presidency	934
199	1960 — U.S. elects Kennedy president	935
200	1961 — U.S.S.R. & U.S. arms race	936
201	1962 — Supreme Court bans school prayer	937
202	1972 — Nixon reelected in landslide	938
203	1973 — Supreme Court legalizes baby killing	939

Copyright 2005 Edward G. Palmer, All Rights Reserved.

Book of Edward—Appendix G

Illustrations, Tables & Lists

204	Seven Founder's statements on governing principles	944
205	God's moral justice v. Injustice v. Court rules	957
206	Seven Democrat societal changes	969
207	Seven facts about moral voting in 2004	974
208	Likened to ten virgins, five wise & five foolish	980
209	Is Hitler in Heaven?	981
210	Seventeen new age beliefs Christians exhibit	984
211	The New School Prayer	988
212	Fifteen lessons in Chapter 21	990
213	The Bible teaches everybody doesn't get to go	991
214	Seven facts from Jesus about showing our light	992
215	Eleven facts from Jesus about being profitable to God	993
216	Eight facts from Jesus about the Nation sorting	994
217	Six reasons Jesus rejects uncaring people	995
218	Jesus' definitions of the wise and the foolish	997
219	Rapture 50% factor	999
220	Three groups judged—one group not judged	1001
221	Three groups judged on the last day	1002
222	One group already passed from death to life	1003
223	Two groups in Heaven—two groups in Hell	1006
224	Christ judges three groups—fourth group gets a pass	1008
225	50% of Christians found wanting	1009
226	50/50 U.S. Christian vote—lawful v. lawless	1010
227	50/50 U.S. national vote—righteous v. unrighteous	1011
228	A dialogue between God & Christ found in Qur'an	1012
229	Seven clear teachings from Christ	1014
230	Christian Church is filled with hypocrites	1017
231	You need a kingdom focus in life	1018
232	Sixty-three facts about the kingdom of God	1019
233	God created Heaven for only a few	1032
234	Ezra prays for mankind	1033
235	God says: "not all will be saved!"	1034
236	God tells Ezra the "signs of end times!"	1035
237	Saved by own choices	1036
238	Condemned by own choices	1036

Copyright 2005 Edward G. Palmer, All Rights Reserved.

Book of Edward—Appendix G

Appendix H
Notes & Bibliography

Bible Translation Notice: Permissions have not been sought to quote from the following Bible translations and the use of all copyrighted citations in this book are considered fair use under the United States copyright laws, which govern the publication of scholarly works. As already noted in the "Forward," a capitalization protocol has been introduced into many cited texts that make a clear distinction between God Almighty [Yahweh] and HIS only begotten human Son, Jesus Christ [Yashua]. Therefore, the cited text may not conform precisely to the printed text used herein in regards to any capitalized characters. Also, some verses are only partially presented for the sake of brevity in this book. The reader is therefore encouraged to examine all Bible citations while reading their own Holy Bible for a more complete and fuller understanding of God's Holy Word.

Forward (piii)

1 — (1611) *The Authorized King James Version* (KJV). Comment: The KJV is in the public domain in the United States and is therefore freely used and quoted by many people. Also, anyone can freely publish the KJV Bible.

2 — (1982) *Holy Bible, New King James Version* (NKJV). Nashville, Tennessee: Thomas Nelson, Inc. Copyright © 1979, 1980, 1982. Comment: The NKJV is an update to the KJV and closely parallels the KJV text. In the author's opinion, the NKJV Bible is an excellent way to enjoy the KJV without getting entangled in trying to comprehend its archaic and outdated English. See chapter 6 for a discussion of the errors found in the KJV.

3 — (1987) *The Amplified Bible* (AMP). La Habra, California: The Zondervan Corporation and the Lockman Foundation.

Notes & Bibliography

4 — (1901) *American Standard Bible* (ASB).

5 — (1970) *New American Standard Bible* (NASB). New York, NY: Catholic Book Publishing Company. Copyright by the Confraternity of Christian Doctrine, Washington DC.

6 — Darby, John Nelson. Public Domain, 1833. *Darby Bible* (DB).

7 — (1917) *Book of Enoch* (ENO). Richard Laurence 1883 Edition.

8 — (1978) *Good News Bible* (GN). Copyright by American Bible Society. New York: Thomas Nelson Publishers. Aka "*The Bible in Today's English Version;*" or, "*Today's English Version.*"

9 — (1978) *Good News Bible; with Deuterocanonicals/Apocrypha* (GNB). Copyright by American Bible Society. New York: Thomas Nelson Publishers. Aka "*The Bible in Today's English Version; with Apocrypha.*"

10 — (1995) *God's Word* (GW). Copyright by the Nations Bible Society. Database © 1997 by NavPress Software at www.WORDsearchBible.com.

11 — Mamre, Mechon (2002) *The Hebrew Bible in English according to the JPS 1917 Edition; HTML Version* (HEB). Internet: Http:www.mechon-mamre.org.

12 — Berlin, Adele and Brettler, March Zvi (Editors) (2004) *Jewish Study Bible* (JSB). Jewish Publication Society, TANAKH Translation. Oxford, New York: Oxford University Press.

13 — (1971) *The Living Bible* (LIV). Wheaton, Illinois: Tyndale House Publishers.

14 — (1996) *Holy Bible, New Living Translation* (NLT). Wheaton, Illinois: Tyndale House Publishers.

15 — (1988) *Microbible* (MB). Copyright by Ellis Enterprises, Inc.

Copyright 2005 Edward G. Palmer, All Rights Reserved.

Book of Edward—Appendix H

Notes & Bibliography

16 — (1988) *Morris Literal Translation* (MLT). Copyright by Ellis Enterprises, Inc., Oklahoma City, OK. See "The Bible Library" software.

17 — Moffatt, James A. R. (1922, 1924, 1925, 1926, 1935, 1950, 1952 and 1954). *The Bible: James Moffatt Translation* (MOF). Final Edition used and Copyrighted in 1994 by Kregel Publications, Grand Rapids, Michigan.

18 — (1984) *The Holy Bible, New International Version* (NIV). Copyright by International Bible Society. Published by Zondervan Bible Publishers.

19 — (1991) *The Holy Bible, New Century Version* (NCV). Aka "*The Everyday Bible.*" Dallas, Texas: Word Publishing. Comment: Excellent modern English translation.

20 — (1985) *The New Jerusalem Bible* (NJB). Copyright by Darton, Longman & Todd Ltd and Doubleday, a division of Bantam Doubleday Dell Publishing.

21 — (1989) *The Revised English Bible* (REB). Copyright by Oxford University Press and Cambridge University Press. Comment: The Revised English Bible is a revision of The New English Bible.

22 — (1952) *Revised Standard Version* (RSV). Copyright by Division of Christian Education of the National Council of Churches of Christ in the United States of America. Zondervan Publishing House.

23 — (1989) *New Revised Standard Version* (NRSV). Copyright by Division of Christian Education of the National Council of Churches of Christ in the United States of America. Zondervan Publishing House.

24 — (1981) *Simple English Translation, New Testament* (SET). Copyright by International Bible Translators, Inc.

25 — Scherman, Nosson and Zlotowitz, Meir (General Editors). (1996) *The Stone Edition, Tanach* (TAN). Brooklyn, New York: Mesorah Publications, Ltd.

Notes & Bibliography

26 — (1988) *Transliterated Bible* (TB). Copyright by Ellis Enterprises, Inc.

27 — Webster, Noah. Public Domain, 1833. *Webster's Bible* (WEB).

28 — Clarke, J. Public Domain, 1909. *Weymouth's New Testament* (WEY).

29 — Young, Robert. Public Domain, 1898. *Young's Literal Translation* (YLT).

Chapter 1

1 — (p10) Media and News reports of the 2000 Federal Elections in the United States indicated a near 50/50 split among voters who would call themselves Christian and that an estimated 90% of the black constituency voted for the Democratic Party presidential candidate.

Chapter 2

1 — (p23) Erwin W. Lutzer's book is an excellent read and explains why you can trust the Holy Bible from a historical translation perspective. Lutzer, however, recommends that you start reading your Bible at John 1:1. This I would take exception to, since it renders confusion over the identity of Jesus Christ from the start. Instead, I recommend you start reading in the Gospels at Matthew 1:1 and then read every red-lettered verse throughout the New Testament. Reading these words of Jesus Christ will bring you clarity, as Jesus never said that he was God. The red-letter verses stand as good theology in and of themselves and only the "Alpha and Omega" verse in Revelations is mis-interpreted as a statement from Jesus. See chapter 10 for a complete study of the phrase "Alpha and Omega" and why that phrase refers to God Almighty not Jesus.

Chapter 3

1 — (p37) Morris, William (1982) *The American Heritage Dictionary: Second College Edition.* Boston, Massachusetts: Houghton Miffin Company.

2 — (p57) Wilkinson, B. (2000). *The PRAYER of JABEZ.* Sisters, Oregon: Multnomah Publishers.

Notes & Bibliography

Chapter 4
None

Chapter 5
None

Chapter 6
1 — (p121) Bryant, T & Et Al (1982) *Today's Dictionary of the Bible.* Carmel, New York: Guideposts.

2 — (p122) Ibid. *The American Heritage Dictionary.*

3 — (p122) Strong, James (1990) *The New Strong'S Exhaustive Concordance Of The Bible.* Atlanta, Georgia: Thomas Nelson Publishers.

Chapter 7
1 — (p134) Ibid.

2 — (p134) Microsoft Word:mac 2001 (1999) *Encarta® World English Dictionary.* Santa Rosa, California: Bloomsbury Publishing Plc.

Chapter 8
1 — (p178) Ibid.

2 — (p180) Reid, David R. (1997) *Hermeneutics Study Guide: Hermeneutics Handout #3.* River Forest, Illinois: Growing Christian Ministries, Inc.

3 — (p191) Ibid.

4 — (p192) Ibid.

5 — (p198) Bristol, Claude M. (1948) *The Magic of Believing* (p64). New York: Pocket Books.

Notes & Bibliography

Chapter 9

1 — (p206) Kazantzakis, Nikos. (1975) *The Last Temptation of Christ*. New York: Simon & Schuster. Translated onto film in 1988 by director Martin Scorsese and stars actor William Dafoe as Jesus Christ. Comment: I never read the book, but the film is a piece of satanic apostasy, which has little resemblance to the Jesus Christ known in the Holy Bible.

2 — (p210) Miles, Jack (2001). *Christ, A Crisis In The Life Of God*. New York: Alfred A. Knopf. Comment: An excellent guide to a full understanding of our modern day Christian mythology. The best intellectual case for the trinity doctrine even if it is filled with apostate misunderstanding and lack of scriptural support from the Holy Bible. Few Christian leaders would openly state what Miles is intellectually forced to conclude having based his theology on the supposition that the trinity doctrine is actual truth. However, his writing reflects an honest intellectual examination of theology having the myth of the trinity doctrine to support.

3 — (p211) Ibid. See page 243-244 of Miles' book.

4 — (p212) Ibid. See page 222 of Miles' book.

5 — (p212) Ibid. See page 224-225 of Miles' book.

6 — (p216) Example. (2000) *The One-Year Chronological Bible*. Wheaton, Illinois:Tyndale House Publishers. Comment: This NLT Bible arranges Scripture according to the time line of actual events. This is in contrast to the canon [out of order] sequence developed by Jerome in the early church. Other translations of the Chronological Bible are available.

7 — (p216) Example. (1981) *The Guideposts Parallel Bible*. Grand Rapids, Michigan: Zondervan Bible Publishers. Comment: This parallel version has the KJV, NIV, LIV and RSV side by side so that all translations can be compared with one another. Other versions have been published and they too make a great study aide. *The Complete Parallel Bible* with Apocryphal/Deuterocanonical Books is also in my library. It has the NRSV, REB, NAB and NJB side by side for comparison.

Notes & Bibliography

8 — (p217) Ibid.

9 — (p217) Ibid. Example: See Strong'S Hebrew Dictionary.

10 — (p217) Ibid. Example: See Strong'S Greek Dictionary.

11 — (p217) Robinson, James M. (Gen. Ed.). (1988). *The Nag Hammadi Library: The Book of Thomas.* New York: HarperCollins Publishers.

12 — (p219) Ibid.

13 — (p223) Ibid.

Chapter 10

1 — (p252) Trinity Episcopal Church, Parkersburg, West Virginia. Web site location on 4/20/03 at http://www.trinity-church.org.

2 — (p253) *Trinity Times Electronic Edition 01/18/99.* Web site location on 4/20/03 at http://www.trinity-church.org/archives/Times_19990118.htm.

3 — (p254) I.E. (10/02) Internet site http://www.av1611.org/nkjv.html.

4 — (p255) (1997) Hagee, John C. (General Editor). *Prophecy Study Bible, New King James Version.* Nashville, Tennessee: Thomas Nelson, Inc.

5 — (p255) John Hagee Ministries on Internet site is http://www.jhm.org.

6 — (p255) Ibid. See page 1429 of *Prophecy Study Bible.*

7 — (p277) Ibid.

8 — (p277) You can research Tertulian on the Internet. One excellent article is located at http://www.newadvent.org/cathen/14520c.htm. This article states that Tertulian "was learned, but careless in his historical statements." From his writings, it is evident that Tertulian possessed limited Scripture writings. I.E. He "did not know James and II Peter."

Notes & Bibliography

9 — (p278) Herbert Armstrong died in 1986. He was the founder of the Worldwide Church of God. Extensive information about him is on the Internet and his organization was often referred to as a cult. I found his radio teachings during my travels fascinating, but I could never match his teachings up with Scripture at the time.

10 — (p278) Ibid.

11 — (p280) See http://www.carm.org/doctrine/trujesus.htm on Internet.

12 — (p283) (1961) *New World Translation* (NWT). Published by the Watchtower Bible and Tract Society of New York. Jehovah Witness. See Luke 23:43 in the NWT and how the comma has been shifted in translation to allow NWT Scripture to agree with Jehovah Witness resurrection and salvation doctrine. <u>Comment</u>: The NWT Bible stands in contrast to many excellent translations and runs counter to the character of Jesus as explained.

13 — (p287) (2001) Hendrickson, Bryn. *Is Jesus The Alpha and Omega?* See Issue No. 11 (Vol. I No. 11) or reference Article #107 when requesting a copy. Published by Growing in the Word Ministries. 7964 Brooklyn Blvd, #208, Brooklyn Park, Minnesota 55445. <u>Comment</u>: Bryn publishes a monthly study and Bible commentary.

14 — (p289) Ibid.

15 — (p289) Ibid. See page 224-225 of Miles' book.

16 — (p295) Ibid.

Chapter 11

1 — (p319) <u>Comment</u>: Research the ordination of V. Gene Robinson, a practicing homosexual to the position of bishop of the New Hampshire diocese by the Episcopalian Church during 2003. Meeting occurred in Minneapolis, Minnesota and volumes of commentaries exist.

2 — (p322) <u>Comment</u>: Research "Gay Pride" on the Internet if interested.

Notes & Bibliography

3 — (p322) <u>Comment</u>: An atheist is attempting to have the words "under God" removed from the Pledge of Allegiance in the United States. A monument of the Ten Commandments was ordered removed from a Court House in Alabama. Both issues are well documented on the Internet and are reflective of the cultural attempt to excise God from society.

4 — (p327) Charles Stanley is on the Internet at http://www.intouch.org.

5 — (p339) (1993) Hill, Paul J. *Should We Defend Born And Unborn Children With Force?* <u>Comment</u>: Paul J. Hill was the first pro-life activist in the United States that was convicted of killing an abortion doctor. His article on 9/5/03 was at http://www.streetpreach.com/Abortion/pjh01.htm. Paul J. Hill advocates the killing of all doctors that willfully kill babies by legalized abortion methods. Kill one person, save thousands is his logic. His arguments and Scripture citations do not carry biblical truth.

6 — (p339) <u>Comment</u>: MSNBC online at http://www.msnbc.com carried extensive articles and commentaries on the Paul J. Hill murder conviction.

7 — (p340) (2003) Bray, Michael. *The Murder of God's Prophet in the Year of Our Lord 2003.* Article dated 2 August 2003 and found on the Internet at http://www.bowiereformation.org/Main/commentary.htm. <u>Comment</u>: The Reverend Bray mistakenly believes Paul J. Hill was a Prophet and that the U.S. executed a man of God doing HIS will. Bray is errant for the reasons cited in Chapter 11.

8 — (p342) Ibid.

9 — (p354) <u>Comment</u>: Extensive writings have been made concerning the U.S. Supreme Courts ruling in 1973 that legalized the killing of babies in the name of female privacy. Whatever else is said about *Roe V. Wade*, one fact is clear and undeniable after 30 years. Over 40 Million babies have been killed or executed. Our society worries about losing a few hundred soldiers who died honorably in the Iraq war. However, it should be hanging its head in shame over needless baby killings. A price will be paid for the shedding of innocent blood and there can be no doubt it is an abomination to God!

Notes & Bibliography

10 — (p367) Ibid. See Jewish Bible references in Forward.

11 — (p367) Ibid. See Holy Bible references in Forward.

12 — (p370) (2001) *The Qur'an*. Text, Translation and Commentary by Abdullah Yusuf Ali. U.S. Edition 2001. Elmhurst, New York: Tahrike Tarsile Qur'an, Inc. Comment: The Koran can be found on the Internet at http://www.koranusa.org. The Qur'an [or Koran] is freely distributed on the Internet as a set of text files. The above version was found online. A second version can be located at http://www.submission.org, which is another Islamic site. This second version is said to be free of the influence of writings outside of the original text as given to the Prophet Mohammed. The first version is said to be influenced by Islamic traditions instead of being simply an accurate translation. I cannot speak to these issues, but have observed that the second version has concluded that all righteous people will go to Heaven regardless of religion. That obviously is what I conclude from our Christian Holy Bible and the teachings of our Lord Jesus Christ.

13 — (p371) The Apostle Edward's definitions based upon his own studies of the three main religions.

Chapter 12

1 — (p383) Mac Hammond Ministries can be found at http://www.lwcc.org.

2 — (p388) Ibid.

3 — (p388) Article printed in the Elk River Star News, Elk River, MN.

4 — (p389) Comment: Tract is the standard type of tract passed out by most Christian Ministries in an attempt to win Christian converts.

5 — (p389) Lakewood Church is located at http://www.Lakewood.cc.

6 — (p415) (1982) *The Guideposts Family Concordance To The Bible*. Guideposts. Carmel, New York: Thomas Nelson, Inc., Publishers.

Notes & Bibliography

Chapter 13

None.

Chapter 14

1 — (p477) (1988) Robinson, James M. (General Editor). *The Nag Hammadi Library in English.* HarperSanFrancisco, a division of Harper Collins Publishers.

2 — (p478) *The Nag Hammadi Library in English: Apocryphon of James.*

3 — (p478) *The Nag Hammadi Library in English: Gospel of Thomas.*

4 — (p480) *The Nag Hammadi Library in English: Gospel of Philip.*

5 — (p481) Ibid.

6 — (p481) (1952) Lewis, CS. *Mere Christianity.* New York, N.Y.: Macmillan Publishing Co., Inc.

7 — (p485) Ibid.

Chapter 15

1 — (p504) Ibid.

2 — (p509) Ibid.

3 — (p524) Ibid.

4 — (p542) Vitamin B17 links for cancer related information are on the Internet at http://www.informcentral.org.

5 — (p542) Dr. David Williams Daily Advantage product can be purchased on the Internet at http://www.drdavidwilliams.com.

Notes & Bibliography

Chapter 16

1 — (p557) Article was published in the Elk River Star News, Elk River, MN circa 1991.

2 — (p600) <u>Comment</u>: George Orwell's well known book titled "1984" dealt with a perceived evil in the form of double speak. Nothing was what it appeared to be. Hence, euphemistic language would be substituted for the evil reality. Instead of the phrase "let's kill babies" — one might use the terminology "let's be pro choice." Indeed, the Orwellian vision of double-speak has materialized and is widely used in the United States. Matthews could preach a lesson on righteousness, while at the same time actually be engaged in wickedness. It was just another application of double-speak.

3 — (p608) Jim Kaseman's AFCM is located at http://www.jkmafcm.org.

4 — (p608) Ibid.

5 — (p609) Ibid.

Chapter 17

1 — (p617) (1991) Johnson, David and VanVoderen, Jeff. *The Subtle Power of Spiritual Abuse.* Minneapolis, Minnesota: Bethany House Publishers. <u>Comment</u>: This is an excellent book that explains what is happening in spiritually abusive churches and what you can do about it.

2 — (p654) Ibid.

3 — (p655) Ibid.

4 — (p661) (1989) Martin, Ernest. *The Tithing Dilemma.* Portland, Oregon: ASK Publications. Online at http://www.askelm.com.

5 — (p661) *The Tithing Dilemma, page 33.*

6 — (p662) *The Tithing Dilemma, page 7.*

Notes & Bibliography

7 — (p662) *The Tithing Dilemma, page 13.*

8 — (p662) *The Tithing Dilemma, page 14.*

9 — (p663) *The Tithing Dilemma, page 25.*

10 — (p663) *The Tithing Dilemma, page 26.*

11 — (p664) *The Tithing Dilemma, page 32.*

12 — (p674) <u>Comment</u>: Religious organizations are officially recognized by the U.S. government and their gifts and donations are then deemed tax deductible gifts if they register with the IRS and declare themselves to be a 501 (c) (3) corporation. As part of IRS Section 501, these corporations and religious organizations must forgo any actions or statements regarding political candidates or parties. Thus, the government muzzles the church in the guise of allowing you to deduct your offerings on the tax form. Hello. What is wrong with that picture? Not surprising, there are many churches arising that refuse to go along with this. It is an interference in religious freedom and unconstitutional.

Chapter 18

1 — (p681) Information on the market for fetal body parts can be found at http://www.letusreason.org/Curren12.htm. The market for "extracted body parts" is greater than for just the fetus as an "unprocessed specimen."

Fetal Body Part	**Body Part Value**
Unprocessed Specimen (8 weeks)	$70.00
Livers (8 weeks)	$15.00
Brains (8 weeks)	$999.00
Brains (8 weeks) – If fragmented	$667.00
Bone Marrow (8 weeks)	$250.00
Ears (8 weeks)	$75.00
Eyes (8 weeks)	$75.00
Pituitary Gland	$300.00
Spinal Cord	$325.00

Notes & Bibliography

The above table of fetal body part values is from the identified link. Given the strong interest in embryonic stem cell research and other areas of fetal research, I believe this data to be valid and if anything will represent outdated low valuations too soon. Do you think the baby boom generation's quest for a fountain of youth is fueling some of the fetal parts research? Do you think a 16 or 24-week specimen is more valuable than an 8-week fetus? My guess is the answer to both questions is yes. Does this outrage you? If not, why doesn't it?

2 — (p682) Byatt, A.S. (Novel). Hwang, David Henry (Screenplay). The 2002 movie is called *Possession* and stars actors Gwyneth Paltrow and Aaron Eckhart. Information is online at http://www.imdb.com/tt0256276/.

3 — (p688) Eastland, Larry L. (June 28, 2004) *The Empty Cradle Will Rock.* This article appeared online at the Wall Street Journal editorial page and was published in the June 2004 issue of *The American Spectator.* The study showed statistics on how abortion is costing the Democrats voters - literally. It is the first political study of *The Roe Effect* that I have read. Mr. Eastland is managing director of LEA Management Group LLC, a public policy research organization. The tables and information contained in this book were obtained from the Wall Street Journal's Online Opinion Edition published at http://www.opinionjournal.com/extra?id=110005277.

4 — (p693) *Merriam-Webster's 11th Collegiate Dictionary.* Version 3.0 of the software was used for the definitions supplied.

5 — (p696) Hill, Napoleon (1979) *The Law of Success (4th Edition) (Chapter 7),* Success Unlimited Edition, Success Unlimited, Inc., Chicago, Illinois.

6 — (p699) Data on the names of the framers of the Constitution obtained on the Internet at http://www.usconstitution.net/constframedata.html.

7 — (p700) Jacoby, Susan (2004) *Freethinkers.* New York, New York, Metropolitan Books, Henry Holt and Company LLC.

8 — (p700) The Virginia Constitution found on the Internet at the following address. Http://www.nhinet.org/ccs/docs/va-1776.htm.

Notes & Bibliography

9 — (p704) *Eclipse of Reason* (1993). "27-minute video produced by former abortionist Bernard Nathanson, M.D. This video documents the termination of a baby boy at five months gestation, as seen by a camera inside the mother's uterus. Charlton Heston introduces the documentary that is sure to ignite the fires of outrage." Note: Descriptive text shown above found at http://shop.store.yahoo.com/americanlifeleague/ecofreasvid.html where the video can be purchase. Since I first viewed this video, little has changed in the nature of abortion politics. That is because too many people remain ignorant of the truth of abortion.

10 — (p705) George R. Tiller clinic located in Wichita, Kansas specializes in late term abortions. Material required by Kansas' "Woman's Right to Know" law is presented at http://www.drtiller.com. Along with the detailed descriptions provided in this book, side-by-side ultrasound photos of the baby at each stage of its development are presented. Detailed information on abortion methods and their medical complications for women are also presented. According to Tom Barrett, who publishes an email newsletter from newsletters@conservativetruth.org, George Tiller is an unabashed abortionist who celebrated Roe v. Wade's 30th anniversary in 2003 by giving away free abortions. Mr. Tiller attends the "Reformation Lutheran Church" in Wichita according to the newsletter. It is a testimony of the lack of respect within various churches for the sanctity of life and its CREATOR.

11 — (p709) Abortion info mega site http://www.abortionfacts.com.

12 — (p709) Abortion info mega site http://www.abortiontv.com.

13 — (p710) Campbell, Stuart (2004), *Scans Uncover Secrets of The Womb*. Found at <u>BBC News World Edition</u> on the Internet at the following link. http://news.bbc.co.uk/2/hi/health/3846525.stm.

14 — (p711) Nova (1999) WGBH Boston Video, *The Miracle of Life*, Boston, Massachusetts. Run time 60 minutes. Product information can be found at Amazon.com and other Internet sites.

15 — (p716) Internet baby picture showing tiny baby held in a doctor's hands. Source is http://www.jesusfolk.com/images/BABY.jpg.

Copyright 2005 Edward G. Palmer, All Rights Reserved.

Book of Edward—Appendix H

Notes & Bibliography

16 — (p716-17) Internet baby picture shows spina bifida surgery on Baby Samuel Armas at 23 weeks gestation. Samuel Armas was born later and is doing fine and the extraordinary picture taken has been circulated around the globe. Additional information on Samuel Adams can be found on the Internet at: http://www.tennessean.com/sii/00/01/09/vandyfetal09.shtml. The *Tennessean* first published the photo of Samuel holding the surgeon's finger. The surgeon removed Samuel's hand from the womb to reposition him for surgery. Spina bifida caused an opening in Samuel's spine, which was then sown shut. Surgery was at the Vanderbilt University Medical Center.

17 — (p719) PETA is the organization of People for the Ethical Treatment of Animals. This organization seeks legislative rights for animals and will revert to violent and destructive actions when they cannot get their way. They clearly believe that animals have a greater right to life than fetuses.

18 — (p720) Amy Richards as told to Amy Barrett (2004). *When One Is Enough.* New York, NY: The New York Times. Article dated July 18, 2004 found online at www.nytimes.com. Commentary and discussion postings found online at www.freerepublic.com.

19 — (p722) Dr. David C. Reardon, Julie Makimaa, & Amy Sobie (2000). *Victims and Victors: Speaking Out About Their Pregnancies, Abortions, and Children Resulting from Sexual Assault.* Acorn Publishing. Found online at http://www.afterabortion.info/Victims.html.

20 — (p722) The Internet site at http://www.afterabortion.info is dedicated to after abortion facts and healing information. Women and their experiences are documenting the real truth about the effects of abortion.

21 — (p728) Article found online at a Kissimmee, Florida Local10 News Internet site. http://www.local10.com/print/3596258/detail.html?use=print. *Teen Gets 50 Years For Sexually Assaulting Girl, 10.*

22-24 (p731-32) Ibid. *Stone's Tanach* page 19 and its footnotes.

25 — (p732) Ibid. *Jewish Study Bible* page 25 footnotes.

Copyright 2005 Edward G. Palmer, All Rights Reserved.

Book of Edward—Appendix H

Notes & Bibliography

26 — (p732) Ibid. The *Talmud* is the authoritative body of Jewish tradition comprising the Mishnah and Gemara.

27 — (p733) Note: Reverend Paul Chaim Benedicta Schenck email letter to Dean Mattila dated July 29, 2004 in reply to question on Genesis 9:6.

28 — (p735) Ibid. Chapter 6, p121.

29 — (p736) Enoch text as found online at Project Timothy. Full Internet address is http://www.projecttimothy.org/book_of_enoch_section_2.htm. The text of the fifth fallen angel teaching mankind to kill the embryo in the womb is found in Richard Laurence's *The Book of Enoch The Prophet* in one chapter earlier than what is shown at the above link [chapter 68 v 69].

30 — (p736) The different chapters and verse references in the two versions of the Book of Enoch reflect different numbering sequences and language nuances. However, both translations contain the same message that the fifth fallen angel Kasyade taught mankind how to kill the embryo in the womb.

31 — (p737) Internet baby picture showing 6-week old fetus. Source is the following: http://abortiontv.com/images/Unborn6Weeks.JPG.

32 — (p738) Hutchinson (2004) Story can be found at http://www.kstp.com. *Doctors Struggle To help Tiny Baby.* Cindy Anderson and Gabriel's story was aired on KSTP-TV on July 28, 2004 at 11:30 a.m.

33 — (p742) The present quote and some Bible references were obtained online at http://www.gospeloflife.net/articles/bible.htm. This site documents Scripture references showing, "The bible teaches that the child in the womb is truly a human child, who even has a relationship with the LORD." Go to site for additional teachings on the subject of life from a Bible perspective.

34 — (p745) Stern, David H. (1998). *Complete Jewish Bible.* Clarksville, Maryland: Jewish New Testament Publications, Inc.

Notes & Bibliography

35 — (p746) This exegesis commentary on Exodus 21:22-25 was found at http://www.pilgrimluth.com/library/Abortion_And_The_Bible.htm.

Chapter 19

1 — (p757) Ibid.

2 — (p760) Quote found at http://www.wisdomquotes.com/001422.html.

3 — (p764) M.S. Word 2001 Dictionary

4 — (p766) From Earl Nightingale's success tape series found at Nightingale-Conant online.

5 — (p771) de Becker, Gavin (1997) *The Gift of Fear.* New York, New York: Little, Brown and Company.

6 — (p773) Article titled: *"A New Kind of Spin the Bottle"* accessed at http://www.oprah.com/pastshows/tows_2002/tows_past20020507_b.jhtml on August 17, 2004.

7 — (p774) Article titled: *"Swaggert Sorry for Remark on 'Killing' Gays"* accessed at http://www.foxnews.com on September 22, 2004.

8 — (p778) Tavis Smiley Show, PBS tpt 17 in Minneapolis-St. Paul on August 26, 2004 at 11:53 p.m. *Interview with Bill Maher.*

9 — (p785) Penner, Clifford and Joyce (1981) *The Gift of Sex.* Dallas, Texas: Word Publishing.

10 — (p787) Rate movies at http://movielens.umn.edu/ on the Internet and learn what your real movie preferences are. This is a University of Minnesota study that encompasses a predictive model. The more movies you rate, the more accurate Movielens will predict whether or not you'll like a movie listed on its site that you have not seen. Links to the Internet Movie Database are present to assist you in your movie analysis. The site is highly predictive for the most part.

Notes & Bibliography

11 — (p792) *"Homosexual S&M part of Christianity?"* Worldnetdaily.com article posted October 8, 2004 cites perverted sexual presentations scheduled for the <u>American Academy of Religion's</u> 2004 (AAR) Annual Meeting in San Antonio. "Two workshops on the sexual themes are being offered by the *Gay Men's Issues in Religion Group*." One paper is titled: "Ecstatic Communion: The Spiritual Dimensions of Leathersexuality." In its abstract, author Justin Tanis of Metropolitan Community Church writes: "All of this [is] based within the framework of a belief in the rights of individuals to erotic self-determination with other consenting adults, rather than apologetics for those practices and lives." The article was accessed at http://www.worldnetdaily.com/news/printer-friendly.asp?ARTICLE_ID=40813 on October 8, 2004. In addition to the many presentations that try to rationalize sexual immorality for Christians, you'd be surprised at who supports the AAR and their efforts. According to the article, the "AAR says it has received support from a number of foundations, including the Lilly Endowment, Inc., The National Endowment for the Humanities, the Henry Luce Foundation, the Booth Ferris Foundation, the William and Flora Hewlett Foundation, and the Fund for the Improvement of Postsecondary Education." AAR is an "organization for professors of religion … with more than 7,500 scholars expected to gather to share research and collaborate on projects." Indeed, there is a distinct difference between such groups and true believers. Think about it long enough and you'll realize why God and Jesus both said: "They worship me in vain!" Especially Ken Stone of Chicago Theological Seminary who claims that Jeremiah 20:7-18 "can be construed more usefully as a kind of S/M encounter." Hello!

12 — (p793) *Hot Showers #7* is a *Hustler video,* produced by Larry Flynt. This pornography video is readily available in adult video stores or for purchase on the Internet. The video has graphic and lurid depictions of women having sex with other women. This is unsuitable viewing for all, but it is an illustration of what I would classify as a "visual" instructional video for the indoctrination of confused teenage females into the immoral realm of lesbianism. There are equally offensive videos on the shelf or Internet for the indoctrination of confused teenage males into homosexuality.

Copyright 2005 Edward G. Palmer, All Rights Reserved.

Book of Edward—Appendix H

Notes & Bibliography

13 — (p794) *In the Cut (2003)*, directed by Jane Campion and starring Meg Ryan and Mark Ruffalo. This is soft-core pornography that couples Meg Ryan in graphic and nude sex acts along with brutal violence in the killing of women. This is unsuitable viewing for all, but it is an illustration of the way that soft-core porn movies are infiltrating the "family" video stores. Stars with name recognition are coupled with graphic sex into a lame movie plot without any redeeming social value. This movie is an example of lascivious behavior on the part of everyone involved.

14 — (p797) Headline reads: *"Muslim cleric wants women of mass destruction,"* (October 9, 2004) Worldnetdaily.com. "Radical cleric Abu Hamza al-Masri is heard urging Muslim women to breed children for the purpose of creating suicide bombers. — This kind of women, when they miss their killed children, they don't go and look for their graves ... they look for their position in paradise, so they become more happy, more anxious to go and see them, they want to sacrifice more and more." The fact is many Muslim clerics and mullahs are not just silent on the issue of mass murder, they are outright advocates of such evil. The Qur'an recognizes Jesus as a prophet and nothing in the Qur'an will save these people from the *woe* Jesus says is coming their way in Matthew 18:6-7. Nothing in the Qur'an alters the condemnation that God imputes to murderers in Rev 21:8.

15 — (p799) Premier Internet merchant at http://www.amazon.com.

16 — (p801) Premier Internet search engine at http://www.google.com.

17 — (p801) As of October 2004, Google did not have a password feature to their search preferences. One should wonder why this is since it is an easy technology to implement. Perhaps it is too easily defeated without setting up a formal user account. In any case, until some viable password methodology is deployed at Google, parents should be aware of the danger of sexually immoral material and the impact it will have on their children.

18 — (p803, 806) Fancher, Bill (2002) *"White Collar Smut Peddlers' Subject of Pro-Family Report."* Article found at http://www.agapepress.org/archive/ 10/afa/312002e.asp and was accessed on October 7, 2004.

Notes & Bibliography

19 — (p804) Burress, Phil (2003), *"It's Not a Privacy Issue!"* Article found at http://www.family.org/cforum/os/p_friendly.cfm?articleurl=/cforum/fosi/pornography/ljaei/a0029600.cfm, which was accessed on October 7, 2004. Burress provides a legal brief on why the distribution of pornography is not protected by the laws even if private use in the home is protected. He lists some of the stats of blue-chip corporation profits.

20 — (p804) Clark, Michael D. (2002), *"CCV Scrutinizes movies at 174 hotels."* Cincinnati, Ohio: The Cincinnati Enquirer. Article found at http://www.enquirer.com/editions/2002/12/17/loc_ccvhotelsurvey17.html and accessed on October 7, 2004.

21 — (p804) The CCV group is sponsoring www.cleanhotels.com "to reward hotels who have chosen not to get involved in the pornography business," according to Phil Burress. On October 7, 2004, the site was not operational and was still being built.

22 — (p806) Associated Press (2004), *"China Offers Rewards for Reporting Porn."* The article states: "China encourages Internet use for education and business but bans sexually oriented content on its own Web sites and tries to block access to foreign sites deemed pornographic or subversive." The article went on to say that China's police ministry offers rewards of up to $240 to people who report such web sites. Comment: It is strange that a communist country realizes the social strain of sexual immorality, but a country like the United States founded on moral grounds does not.

23 — (p806) Ibid.

24 — (p806-807) Ibid.

25 — (p810) Parker, Laurie (2004), *"Church Sign Says God Hates."* Article found at http://www.whnt19.com/global/story.asp?/s=2403511&ClientType=Printable. Accessed on October 9, 2004. WHNT News 19 Channel article describes a sign in front of the St. Luke Missionary Baptist Church, which is close to the Metropolitan Community Church in Huntsville, a predominantly Gay congregation just down the road from the former.

Notes & Bibliography

26 — (p813) Ibid. *The Gift of Sex (p230).*

27 — (p815) London, England (2004). *"Study: One in 100 adults asexual."* A survey by Anthony Bogaert, a psychologist and human sexuality expert at Brock University in St. Catherines, Ontario conducted the study and found an estimated 1% of the people to be asexual and not interested in sex. He also stated the there was a 3% homosexual population.

28 — (p816) Thompson, Jenny (2004) *"Men: Is medicine turning you into a woman?"* Health Science Institute Newsletter. To subscribe to this free premier newsletter, email HSIResearch@healthiernews.com. Author describes Dr. Sear's discoveries that men are in a "vicious cycle of decreasing testosterone and increasing estrogen. You start to look and feel more like a woman but your mind, your culture, still expect you to be a man." The evidence is in and males are having serious hormone issues and this may be one factor in the confused sexual state of males and females.

29 — (p819) Mackinnon, Grace (2004). *"Masturbation: Mortal Sin?"* Found online at http://catholiceducation.org/articles/religion/rre0706.html. Article was accessed on 9/11/04. Writer cites the Catechism of the Catholic Church (CCC# 2352) as a reference source. "Both the Magisterium of the Church, in the course of constant tradition, and the moral sense of the faithful have been in no doubt and have firmly maintained that masturbation is an intrinsically and gravely disordered action."

30 — (p822) Fox, Douglas (2003). Adelaide, Australia. *"Masturbating may protect against prostate cancer."* Article accessed on 9/11/2004 and found at http://www.newscientist.com/news/print.jsp?id=ns99993942.

31 — (p824-825) Johanson, Sue (2004). Provides sex education devoid of spiritual aspects but takes care to invoke sanitation issues of health. Teaches masturbation is acceptable and has instructional lessons on line for a variety of sex topics. Http://www.milkandcookies.com/print.php?sid=1861 is an explanation for women on how to perform oral sex. This Canadian sex therapist is featured prominently on the Oxygen woman's cable network and has a regular show called "Sex Talk With Sue." Caution: graphic dialogue.

Copyright 2005 Edward G. Palmer, All Rights Reserved.

Book of Edward—Appendix H

Notes & Bibliography

32 — (p825) Ibid. *The Gift of Sex (p230-236)*.

33 — (p825) Male masturbation is taught at http://www.jackinworld.com.

34 — (p825) Female masturbation is taught at http://www.clitical.com.

35 — (p826) Ibid. *The Gift of Sex (p73)*.

36 — (p828) Ibid. *The Gift of Sex (p227-230)*. Note: Penners used the NIV, NASB and LIV Bibles.

37 — (p829) Ibid. *The Gift of Sex (p229)*.

38 — (p832) Boston.com (2004) *"Couple allegedly has sex at the Alamo."* Article at http://www.boston.com/news/nation/articles/2004/10/11/couple_alledgedly_have_sex_at_the_alamo?mode=PF accessed on 10/11/2004. "The [police] report said Kristine Nissel, 18, and Matthew Hotard, 19, were partially clad when the officer apprehended them after several tourists watched the couple and became upset. The pair, both active-duty members of the 232nd Medical Battalion stationed at Fort Sam Houston, was charged with public lewdness ... Bond was set for each at $800."

39 — (p832) Fox News Join the Debate. (2004) *"Streaker Shock."* Article at http://www.foxnews.com/printer_friendly_story/0,3566,77925,00.html and accessed on 10/16/2004. "In response to being banned from his graduation ceremonies, one Pennsylvania high school student chose to wear his birthday suit instead of his cap and gown. Now the teen faces six months to two years of jail time for his streaking stunt."

40 — (p832) WBOC-TV16 (2004). *"Old school days long gone, but not forgotten; Congressman's streaking stunt exposed."* Article accessed on 10/12/2004 and found at http://www.wboc.com/global/story.asp?=2416017&ClientType=Printable. Article states, "Democrats are circulating old newspaper clippings of a 1974 college streaking stunt staged by hundreds of students at what was then called Southwest Texas State University."

41 — (p832) Real Cancun, The (2003). Genre: Documentary per Imdb.com.

Notes & Bibliography

42 — (p833) Baker, Andrew R. (2000). *"Cohabitation fails as test for marriage."* Found at http://www.catholic.net/rcc/Periodicals/HPR/May00/marriage.html and accessed on 9/10/2004. Author cites the many studies that show cohabitation is problematic and even a prelude to later marriage failure. "A University of Wisconsin survey found that marriages preceded by living together have a 50% higher disruption rate (divorce or separation) that marriages without premarital cohabitation."

43 — (p834, 842) National Marriage Project (2002). *"The Second Edition of Should We Live Together."* Found online at http//marriage.rutgers.edu/Publications/SWLT@%20TEXT.htm and accessed on 9/10/2004. Among a long list of citations, the study points out "No positive contribution of cohabitation to marriage has ever been found."

44 — (p836) Ibid. Merriam-Webster.

45 — (p841) Males experiencing sexual complications and or ED (erectile dysfunction) can find natural remedies from Dr. Al Sears, M.D. a specialist in male health. You can find information at http://www.vitalmax.com or call the toll free number 800-815-5151 valid as of October 21, 2004. In fact there are many sources of alternative medicine approaches to this issue that are a lot safer that taken prescription drugs that increase nitric oxide levels.

46 — (p846) Ibid. Strong'S Concordance.

47 — (p849) CBSNEWS.com (2004). *"Rosie To Marry Girlfriend."* Article found at http://www.cbsnews.com/stories/2004/02/26/entertainment/printable602385.shtml and accessed on 2/26/04. Discusses Rosie O'Donnell's opinion of Gay marriage of which she is an advocate and her plans to marry her longtime girlfriend Kelli Carpenter.

48 — (p850) U.S. Census Bureau (2003). *"Married-Couple and Unmarried-Partner Households: 2000."* The full report can be accessed online at the Census Bureau site located at http://www.census.gov. Data from the 2000 Census clearly pegs the Gay population at 1% or less.

Notes & Bibliography

49 — (p850) Meredith, J. L. (1980). *Meredith's Book of Bible Lists (p176).* Minneapolis: Bethany Fellowship, Inc. Bible references are from the King James Version.

50 — (p851) Ibid. U.S. Census Bureau Data

51 — (p853) Ibid.

52 — (p854) ABC NEWS (2004). *"Primetime Live Poll: American Sex Survey."* Online at http://abcnews.go.com/Primetime/print?id=156921 and accessed on 10/22/2004.

53 — (p854) CBS NEWS (2004). *"For Teens, Sex & Drugs Go Together."* Online at http://www.cbsnews.com/stories/2004/08/19/national/printable 637118.shtml and accessed on 8/19/2004.

54 — (p855) MIRROR.CO.UK (2004). *"Girl, 12, Blamed by Judge for Sex Attack."* Online at http://www.mirror.co.uk/printable_version?method= printable_version_mirror&objectid=14615774&sitrid=50143 and accessed on 8/25/2004.

55 — (p855) FOX NEWS (2004). *"On Breastfeeding, Rights and Good Manners."* Online at http://www.foxnews.com/printer_friendly_story/0, 3566,129908,00.html and accessed on 8/25/2004.

56 — (p856) WorldNetDaily (2004). *"Aborted baby's head left inside woman."* Online at http://www.worldnetdaily.com/news/printer-friendly.asp ?ARTICLE_ID=40024.

57 — (p857) IRISH EXAMINER (2004). *"Bishop: Anglican Church may be beyond repair."* Online at http://www.irishexaminer.com/breaking/ email/printer.asp?j=120021412&p=yzxxzzyy8&n=120022172&x= and accessed on 10/8/2004. Article discusses the Anglican Church split caused by the U.S. Episcopal branch ordaining an active Gay bishop.

58 — (p857) FOX NEWS (2004). *"Anglican Panel Blasts Episcopal Church for Gay Stance."* Online at http://www.foxnews.com/printer

Notes & Bibliography

_friendly_story/0,3566,135724,00.html and accessed on 10/18/2004. Article states, "Worldwide, Anglican conservatives are heavily in the majority. A 1998 conference of all Anglican bishops declared Gay practices 'incompatible with Scripture' and opposed Gay ordinations and same-sex blessings in a 526-70 vote with 45 abstentions."

59 — (p858) FOX NEWS (2004). *"Housewives Too Hot for Advertisers."* Online at http://www.foxnews.com/printer_friendly_story/0,3566,135873,00.html and accessed on 10/19/2004. Describes how ABC's "Desperate Housewives" have crossed the decency threshold because of racy content and the fact that advertisers are pulling away from supporting the show.

60 — (p858) Medical News Today (2004). *"Sexually Transmitted Infections continue to increase during 2003 in UK."* Accessed on 7/27/2004 and found at http://www.medicalnewstoday.com/printerfriendlynews.php?/newsid=11335.

61 — (p858) The Desert Sun (2004). *"Not a simple answer for desert's syphilis problem."* Online at http://www.thedesertsun.com/news/stories/2004/health/20041003031904.shtml and accessed on 10/4/2004. Article describes the syphilis epidemic in Palm Spring, California and states it is the highest of any city in the U.S.

62 — (p859) WIRED (2004). *"Google vs. Evil."* Accessed on 10/7/2004 and online at http://www.wired.com/wired/archive/11.01/google_pr.html. Article discusses the moral compromises Google's founders find they are in trying to resolve the corporate core value statement of "Don't be evil." An estimated 80% of all Internet searches are now done by Google. Therefore, for the moment, its search technology is now foundational to the Internet.

63 — (p860) Ibid. *Today's Dictionary of The Bible (p35).*

64 — (p861) Ibid. *Today's Dictionary of The Bible (p428).*

65 — (p863) Ibid. *Meredith's Book of Bible Lists (p177).*

66 — (p877) Ibid. *The Gift of Sex (p78-80).*

Notes & Bibliography

67 — (p877) White, Barry -song. *"Can't Get Enough Of Your Love, Babe."* Lyrics and music can be found online at http://www.lyricsondemand.com.

68 — (p879) *The Gift of Sex* (p79) Note: "Helen Singer Kaplan, *The New Sex Therapy* (New York: Brunner/Mazel, 1974), pp. 13-15."

69 — (p879) Carmen, Eric –song. *"Make Me Lose Control."* Lyrics and music can be found online at http://www.lyricsondemand.com.

70 — (p881) Ibid. *Merriam-Webster.*

71 — (p881) *"Asia lags behind Europe in sex, reveals Durex Survey."* Found at http://www.hindustantimes.com/181_1055140,00050004.htm and accessed on 10/13/2004. Article sites frequency of sex in different countries.

72 — (p882) *"We're Not In The Mood."* Found at http://www.nomarriage.Com/articlesexless.html and accessed on 10/27/2004.

73 — (p882) Note: Comment found in *"We're Not In The Mood"* article.

74 — (p883) Holstein, Lana, M.D. *"How To Have Magnificent Sex."* Info can be found at http://www.lanaholsteinmd.com.

75 — (p883) Gray, John, Dr. *"Men are from Mars, Women are from Venus."* Found online at http://www.marsvenus.com.

Chapter 20

1 — (p898) USA TODAY survey states that <u>the most important issue</u> cited by 22% of the 2004 voters was "Moral Values." Survey results found at http://www.usatoday.com/news/graphics/election2004_week/exitpolls/flash.htm and accessed on 11/3/2004. Bush beat Kerry in the total popular vote with 51% of the vote compared to Kerry's 48%.

2 — (p898) StarTribune Editorial Page A24, Friday November 5, 2004. *"Faith works in all ways"* by Cindy Marty, Bloomington, MN.

Notes & Bibliography

3 — (p899, 906) Ibid. Merriam-Webster.

4 — (p901) Note: States that voted for Bush were called "Red States" and those that voted for Kerry were called "Blue States." However, when a county map of the United States is viewed, the entire United States appears as a sea of red from coast to coast. Only large metro areas in the Blue States allowed Kerry to carry those states. For example, New York State is almost entirely Red except for New York City. Minnesota is almost entirely Red except for Minneapolis, St. Paul and Duluth. It appears that a significant moral difference exists between large metro areas and the rest of the country.

5 — (p901) THE WEEKLY STANDARD (2004). *"Rove's Secret Weapon: Stupid People."* Found online at http://www.theweeklystandard.com and accessed on 11/13/2004.

6 — (p902) USA TODAY. Race/Ethnicity Voter Graphic shows 89% of blacks voted for Kerry and 11% voted for Bush. Found at http://www.usatoday.com/news/graphics/election2004_week/exitpolls/flash.htm and accessed on 11/3/2004.

7 — (p902) Associated Press, October 19, 2004. *"Poll: Bush Doubles Support Among Blacks."* Article found on Yahoo News. "Exit polls in 2000 showed Gore winning 90 percent of the black vote, with Bush at 9 percent — the lowest support for a Republican presidential candidate since Barry Goldwater garnered 6 percent in 1964."

8 — (p902) Parker, Star (2004). *"How GOP can win the black vote."* Found at http://www.worldnetdaily.com/news/article.asp?ARTICLE_ID=41364 and accessed on 11/13/2004. Parker states: "Black Christians still vote overwhelmingly Democratic."

9 — (p903) FREEDOM WORKS (2002). *"Russia's Flat Tax Reform."* Found at http://www.freedomworks.org/processor/printer.php?/issue_id=890 and accessed on 11/13/2004. "Since January 1, 2001, Russians have enjoyed a 13 percent flat tax ... Revenue has grown as a result following the Laffer Curve: lower marginal tax rates produce higher [tax] revenues."

Notes & Bibliography

10 — (p907) Shamir, Shlomo, Haaretz Correspondent (2004). *"Kerry wins 78% of Jewish vote; Bush wins 22%."* Found at http://www.haaretzdaily.com/hasen/objects/pages/PrintArticleEn.jhtml?/itemNo=497277 and accessed on 11/13/2004. Note: Article states that at 78%, Kerry won just 2% less than Al Gore did in the 2000 election. Bush's 22% is a 3% gain over the 19% he received in the 2000 election.

11 — (p907) Gallup Poll News Service (2004). *"How Americans Voted."* Found at http://www.gallup.com/poll/content/print.aspx?/ci=13957 and accessed on 11/2/2004. Note: This is a statistical analysis of voting, which also compared the 2000 election results to the 2004 results.

12 — (p909-910) Religion ETHICS Newsletter (2004). *"Perspectives: Election 2004 Analysis (Episode no. 810)."* Found at http://www.pbs.org/wnet/religionandethics/week810/perspectives.html and accessed on 11/15/2004. This comprehensive PBS news article features Bob Abernethy, as anchor; Professor John Green, a leading expert on religion and politics from the Ray C. Bliss Center for Applied Politics, University of Akron and Kim Lawton from RELIGION & ETHICS NEWSWEEKLY with the exit polls conducted on Election Day by Edison Media Research and Mitofsky International.

13 — (p911) Ibid. U.S. Census Report *"Married-Couple and Unmarried-Partner Households: 2000."* Note: This is extrapolated data from tables 2 and 4 of the report. Table 2 indicates that 301,026 same sex households have male partners and 293,365 same sex households have female partners. Table 4 indicates an average of 22.5% of the male households have kids under 18 and an average of 33.5% of female households have kids under 18. Math is 301,026 x .225 + 293,365 x .335 equals a total of 166,007 underage kids being raised by Gay households.

14 — (p912) FOXNEWS with Chris Wallace as seen on KSMP-TV Fox 9 in Minneapolis on 11/14/2004. In his interview with Chris Wallace, Senate Leader Bill Frist stated, "Morals never changes." Note: This is correct thinking as it is God Almighty who has defined moral values, not mankind.

Notes & Bibliography

15 — (p914) Kesler, Charles R. (1961) *The Federalist Papers* (p32-33). New York, New York: Signet Classic Books.

16 — (p918) Note: The concept of Red States vs. Blue States is deceptive in its presentation. When the United States is viewed as a County Map, almost the entire nation is in "red" save for very large metro areas. This "Red" county-nation map can be found at http://www.newsmax.com.

17 — (p918) Note: List shown are some of the ideas contained in an email my friend Dean received from rorlb@fgn.net and attributed to an email titled *"Separation of Church & State"* written by C-log reader Jim Moore on or about 8/31/2004. The list was not reprinted verbatim, but the originator of the basic thoughts is hereby acknowledged.

18 — (p922) Equal Marriage for same-sex couples (2004). *"Saskatchewan sends message of hope."* Found at http://www.samesexmarriage.ca and accessed on 11/16/2004. Article states, "Saskatchewan became Canada's 7th region to legalize same-sex marriage, this morning, when a court ordered the province to end discrimination against Gay and lesbian couples." In a related article it states *"New York accepts Canadian Gay marriages."*

19 — (p922) WORLDNETDAILY (2004). *"Bible as Hate Speech signed into law."* Found at http://www.worldnetdaily.com/news/article.asp?/ARTICLE_ID=38268 and accessed on 11/16/2004. Article quotes Liberal Party Parliament member John Mckay saying, "Anybody who has views on homosexuality that differ from Svend Robinson's will be exposed rather dramatically to the joys of the Criminal Code [in Canada]." In a related article, a Canadian man was fined $5,000 for taking out a newspaper ad citing Scriptures that condemned homosexuality. Another Canadian was fined $5,000 for refusal to print homosexual materials at his Christian business. Canada's activist homosexual organization EGALE explained it this way. "There's a huge difference between someone being allowed to practice their religion and taking out ads in the newspaper saying that Gay and lesbian people are sick and immoral," said EGALE's Vance. "There is a line there, and it's been crossed." Comment: Christians practicing their faith are required to rebuke sin and wickedness. The only thing Canada did was to abridge freedom of speech and sanctify immorality. *Woe to Canada!*

Notes & Bibliography

20 — (p935-939) Daniel, Clifton, Editor in Chief (1987) *Chronicle of the 20th Century*. Mount Kisco, New York: Chronicle Publications Inc. Note: All events listed in the table are newspaper headlines and articles contained in the historical record of this book. See year and date for details.

21 — (p928) Note: Kennedy's acceptance speech is found at http://www.Americanrhetoric.com/speeches/JFK1960dnc.htm and was accessed on 11/19/2004. It is also found at the *American Presidency Project* online where details of all presidential elections are found. This latter resource is an excellent one for students of the U.S. presidency.

22 — (p929) Cass, Connie, AP Writer (2004). *"Addiction to porn destroying lives, Senate told."* Article found at http://www.sfgate.com and accessed on 11/18/2004.

23 — (p930) Hayes, Matt (2004). *"Combating Judicial Political Activism."* Found at http://www.foxnews.com and accessed on 11/13/2004. "Judges do their jobs with surprisingly few checks on the decisions they make, and appellate courts give judges ... wide latitude in sentencing."

24 — (p930) Holland, Gina, AP Writer (2004). *"Supreme Court justice gets racy on talk circuit."* Found at http://www.sfgate.com and accessed on 10/1/2004. "While making the point that judges can have personal moral judgments, it is not the judge's role to impose them on citizens."

25 — (p930) *1960 Democratic Platform* at http://www.presidency.ucsb.edu.

26 — (p941) Note: George Washington's *First Thanksgiving Proclamation* can be found at http://press-pubs.uchicago.edu/founders/documents/amendI_religions54.html and several other places. Accessed on 11/24/2004.

27 — (p950) Note: John Adams quotes are found at http://marksquotes.com/Founding-Fathers/Adams/index2.htm and were accessed on 9/5/2004.

28 — (p953) John Quincy Adams quote found at http://www.quoteworld.Org/search.php?/thetext=john+adams and accessed on 9/5/2004.

Notes & Bibliography

29 — (p953) John Quincy Adams quote found at http://christianamerica.com/jqaquotes.htm and accessed on 9/5/2004.

30 — (p971) Grafton, John, Editor (2000) *The Declaration of Independence and Other Great Documents of American History 1775-1865.* Mineola, New York: Dover Publications, Inc.

31 — (p971) Worldnetdaily.Com (2004). *"ACLU threatens abstinence program."* Found at http://www.worldnetdaily.com/news/article.asp?ARTICLE_ID=41544 and accessed on 11/19/2004. Note: State of Louisiana is being threatened with a lawsuit because they have a website promoting abstinence and a 15 year old girl has a testimonial on the site in which she "thanks God" for helping her keep her virginity until marriage.

32 — (p974) SFGATE.COM (2004). *"EU officials implore new immigrants to learn 'European values.'"* Found at www.sfgate.com and accessed on 11/19/2004. Note: EU officials want the melting pot idea to take hold. And they want to hold on to their existing values. Watch what happens as they absorb the "moral" Muslims. Do you think they can get them to not vote for "their morals?" They should therefore codify into their Constitution what they think their EU morals are supposed to be.

33 — (p974) Ostling, Richard N., AP Religion Writer (2004). *"Election Reinforces U.S. Religious Divide."* Found at http://cnn.netscape.cnn.com/news/story.jsp?/floc=ne-election-11-115&flok=FF-APO-1130&idq=/ff/story/0001/20041104/1641791322.htm&sc=1130. Note: Good luck on that URL. It may be better to search at cnn.netscape.cnn.com for the story title. Accessed on 11/4/2004. Also note that various stats from different sources quoted may not match up to one another due to different sample groups.

Chapter 21

1 — (p979) Green, Steve — Song: *People Need The Lord.* Lyrics found online at http://www.stlyrics.com.

2 — (p980) Walsch, Neale Donald (1996). *Conversations with God, *An Uncommon Dialogue*, Book 1.* New York: G.P. Putnam's Sons.

Notes & Bibliography

3 — (p980) Ibid. Walsch's Book 1, p61.

4 — (p981) Ibid. Walsch's Book 1, p3.

5 — (p981) Ibid. Walsch's Book 1, p8.

6 — (p981) Ibid. Walsch's Book 1, p41.

7 — (p981) Ibid. Walsch's Book 1, p133.

8 — (p981) Ibid. Walsch's Book 1, p135.

9 — (p982) Ibid. Walsch's Book 1, p135.

10 — (p982) Ibid. Walsch's Book 1, p136.

11 — (p982) Ibid. Walsch's Book 1, p138.

12 — (p982) Ibid. Walsch's Book 1, p149.

13 — (p982) Ibid. Walsch's Book 1, p143.

14 — (p982) Ibid. Walsch's Book 1, p153.

15 — (p982) Ibid. Walsch's Book 1, p155.

16 — (p982) Ibid. Walsch's Book 1, p160.

17 — (p983) Ibid. Walsch's Book 1, p162.

18 — (p983) Ibid. Walsch's Book 1, p174.

19 — (p983) Ibid. Walsch's Book 1, p175.

20 — (p983) Ibid. Walsch's Book 1, p183.

21 — (p983) Ibid. Walsch's Book 1, p184.

Notes & Bibliography

22 — (p983) Ibid. Walsch's Book 1, p187.

23 — (p983) Ibid. Walsch's Book 1, p193.

24 — (p983-84) Ibid. Walsch's Book 1, p194.

25 — (p984) Ibid. Walsch's Book 1, p205.

26 — (p985) Fox News.com (2004). *"Banned from Showing Students the Declaration of Independence."* Article found online at http://www.foxnews.Com/printer-friendly-story/0,3566,140042,00.html and accessed on 12/1/2004.

27 — (p986) AgapePress.org (2004). *"Attorney Hopes Texas Court Will Uphold Pastor's Rights."* Article found online at http://www.agapepress.org and was accessed on 12/2/2004.

28 — (p986) NewsMax.com (2004). *"Pelosi: Marriage Amendment Discriminates Against Gays."* Article found at http://www.newsmax.com and accessed on 12/5/2004.

29 — (p986) Ostling, Richard N., AP News (2004). *"Methodist Jury Convicts Lesbian Minister."* Available at various Internet sites such as http://www.agapepress.org and accessed on 12/2/2004.

30 — (p987) WorldNetDaily.com (2004). *"Principal apologizes for prayer."* Article found at http://www.worldnetdaily.com/news/article.asp?/ARTICLE_ID=41699 and accessed on 11/20/2004.

31 — (p988) Note: The *New School Prayer* started circulating around the Internet after the Columbine High School shootings and eloquently speaks to the upside down nature of our debased public school system.

32 — (p996) CNSNEWS.COM (2004). *"Why Democrats Will Continue Losing the 'Moral Values' Vote."* Found at http://www.cnsnews.com and accessed on 12/7/2004. Commentary by Sterling Rome states:

Notes & Bibliography

"Gore railed about representing the 'people versus the powerful' [in 2000] but we later found out that he doesn't give any money to charity. ... Hypocrisy like this is routinely dismissed by the Democrats."

33 — (p1000) Clair, Christopher (2004). *"Burke's quotation does nothing but triumph."* Source: http://scotlandonsunday.scotsman.com/entertainment.cfm?id=1393992004 and accessed on 12/5/2004. Note: Edmund Burke was a famous 18th century political philosopher. The phrase, which is not found in Burke's writings, is widely attributed to him according to this article.

34 — (p1001) AP NEWS (2004). *"March Against Same-Sex Marriage Uses King Quote."* Found at http://www.newsmax.com/archives/ic/2004/12/10/143949.shtml and accessed on 12/10/2004.

35 — (p1012) Ali, Abdullah Yusuf (2001). *The Qur'an* (Text, Translation and Commentary). Elmhurst, New York: Tahrike Tarsile Qur'an, Inc. Note: the phrase "Surah" simply means "book." In the section quoted, it is simply referencing Book 5, Verses 116-117. Ergo, "Surah 5:116-117." In some Islam books, the word appears as "Sura" v. "Surah." Also, the Qur'an itself may appear as "Quran" or "Koran."

36 — (p1015) ABC News (2004). *"Sexual Abuse in the Amish Community."* Found at http://abcnews.go.com/2020/print?id=316371 and accessed on 12/11/2004. Note: Elizabeth Vargas' report exposed the hellish life of a woman who endured a childhood of repeated rape by her brothers.

Appendix I
Bible Verse Cross Reference

Over 1,367 God Inspired Scripture References!

Read the book and the God inspired scriptures in the order that God gave them to me in each chapter. After you've read the book, use this Bible verse cross-reference as a study aid. Compare Bible verses of interest to the writings and spiritual explanations contained in this book. I want to acknowledge and thank my dear friend Dean Mattila for his work for the FATHER in compiling this reference.

The Bible verses shown below are cited in part, in whole or else they are discussed in the conversation on the pages listed. Where successive verses are listed individually, those verses are cited and discussed individually within the conversation of this book, even on the same page. Where a range of verses is cited, the verses are discussed or presented collectively for your study. The Apostle Edward

ACTS	Page
1:3	116
1:8	12, 306, 1050
1:22	124
1:26	123
2:14-36	124
2:15-21	viii
2:21	5
2:32-33	256, 270, 276
4:19	360
5:3	256

Bible Verse Cross Reference

5:3-4	266, 276
5:29	634
5:32	635
7:55-60	280
7:58	31
8:3	31
8:37	1047
9:4	31
9:5	31
9:15	31
9:21	32
9:22	32
10:34-35	3, 1011, 1012, 1057, 1060
10:47	1047
10:47-48	556
11:24	362
13:2	123
13:9-10	35
13:22	37, 896, 976, 1038
13:27	653
13:44	653
14:22	1029
15:8	29
17:11	94
17:24	16, 27
19:3-4	1046
22:15-16	1047
22:16	555
26:16	593

AMOS	Page
1:13	742
1:13-15	860
5:18-20	791, 792

Copyright 2005 Edward G. Palmer, All Rights Reserved.

Book of Edward—Appendix I

Bible Verse Cross Reference

COLOSSIANS	Page
1:2	25
1:28	100, 777
2:16-17	628, 646
3:2	926
3:3	630
3:5-7	796, 836, 839
3:8-10	375
4:3	452

1 CORINTHIANS	Page
1:1-2	280
1:2	25
3:1-3	397
3:9	16
3:15	279
3:16	17
3:17	17
3:22	123
4:20	1030
5:9-10	46
5:9-11	749
5:9-13	359
5:11	545, 795
5:11-13	47
5:12	598
6:6	568
6:9	814, 839
6:9-10	38, 39, 644, 991, 1030
6:9-11	361
6:10	991
6:12	657
6:19	515, 648
7:2-5	823
7:3-5	557
7:10-11	923

Copyright 2005 Edward G. Palmer, All Rights Reserved.

Book of Edward—Appendix I

Bible Verse Cross Reference

8:6	305, 306, 1049, 1053
10:13	443, 823, 843, 844
10:20	597
10:31	896, 976, 1038
11:3	1064
11:18-21	950
12:3	6
12:4-6	256, 271, 276
12:7-10	552
12:28	110
12:30	554
13	683, 729
13:4-7	729
13:4-13	678
13:12	360
13:13	1040
14:5	554
14:6	553
14:18	553
14:22-23	553
14:33	295
14:39	553
15:24	1030
15:33	445, 589
15:34	395, 414
15:50	1030

2 CORINTHIANS	Page
1:1	25
1:3-4	499
1:4	416
1:18	941
1:20	291
3:3	423
4:2	547
5:6-8	422

Bible Verse Cross Reference

5:13	219
6:14	161, 597, 949
6:16	474
8:9	661
9:7	670
10:3	423
11:13-15	545, 595
11:15	149
12:6	102
12:9	102
12:21	768, 807, 839
13:1-6	124
13:11	926
13:14	256, 271, 276

1 CHRONICLES	Page
4:10	57
12:15	264
12:32	200
16:23	382
29:29	264

2 CHRONICLES	Page
7:14	945
16:9	371, 429
20:34	264
26:5	200

DANIEL	Page
2:20-23	176
5:5-7	90
5:25-28	91
5:27	89, 1009
5:30	91

Copyright 2005 Edward G. Palmer, All Rights Reserved.

Book of Edward—Appendix I

Bible Verse Cross Reference

DEUTERONOMY	Page
4:6	171
4:29	1058
5:6-21	627
5:7-21	19-20
5:12	649
5:17	348
5:24	11
5:24-27	318
5:28-29	319
5:29	306, 1051
6:1-11:32	627
6:4	1048
7:15	519
12:1-28	628
12:1-16:17	626, 627
12:29-13:18	628
12:32	152, 193
13:5	48, 306, 1050
14:1-21	628
14:22-29	584, 615, 618, 620, 623, 628, 1042, 1065
14:23	620
14:24	620
14:25	620
14:26	620
14:27	620
14:28	620
14:29	620
15:1-11	628
15:12-18	628
15:19-23	628
16:1-17	628
16:18-20:20	627
17:7	48, 306, 1050
17:12	48
18:9	949

Bible Verse Cross Reference

18:20	347
19:10	714
19:19	48, 1050
21:1-26:19	627
21:18-21	48, 1050
22:20-21	49, 640
22:20-24	1050
22:22	49
22:23-24	49
22:25-27	721
24:5	876
24:7	49, 1050
24:16	516
27:26	625
29:27	864
30:8-20	138
30:19	131, 132, 137, 724
32:4	897
32:28	200
32:35	348
32:36	113
34:7	439

ECCLESIASTES	Page
3:4	818
3:8	743, 745
3:11	381
3:15	335
5:15	746
7:14	538
11:14	313
12:12	368
12:13-14	369

Bible Verse Cross Reference

EPHESIANS	Page
1:1	25
1:2-14	256, 272, 276
2:15	631, 632, 643
2:18	256, 273, 276
2:18-22	17
2:19-20	124
3:5	124
3:13	378
4:5	1046, 1047
4:4-6	256, 273, 276
4:11	124
4:19-20	807
4:21-23	30, 71
4:28	141
5:5	836
5:9	96
5:11	795
5:11-12	547, 567
5:28	823
5:22-33	884
5:33	884
6:13	531

2 ESDRAS	Page
1:25	740
2:32	740
8:1-3	453
8:7-11	712
8:1-40	1032-1034
8:41-9:22	1034-1037
14:34	740

ESTHER	Page
16:4	967

Copyright 2005 Edward G. Palmer, All Rights Reserved.

Book of Edward—Appendix I

Bible Verse Cross Reference

EXODUS	Page
2:11-14	343
2:12	344
2:15	344
3:4	59
15:26	519
16:23	650
16:25-26	650
16:29	650
20:3-7	243
20:5	865
20:10-11	650
20:13	348
20:20	320, 369
21	684, 745
21:22-25	353, 678, 683, 684, 691, 745, 746, 1059
21:23	646
22:16	646
23:2	306, 797, 1050
23:25-26	519
23:26	746
31:3	171
31:13	646
31:15, 16, 17	650
33:11	1049
33:19	381, 492
33:20	317
33:21-23	318
33:34-35	174
35:2	650
35:3	650
35:31-34	171

EZEKIEL	Page
7:3-4	374, 686, 890
7:8-9	320

Copyright 2005 Edward G. Palmer, All Rights Reserved.

Book of Edward—Appendix I

Bible Verse Cross Reference

8:17	321
11:12	321
13:2	321
13:3	791
13:6	321
13:19	321
13:22	321
13:23	88
14:14	414
18	1048, 1058
18:4	29, 731, 1051, 1057
18:4-32	410
18:9	414
18:17-18	1062
18:21	414
18:30	28, 1063
18:31	414, 1063
18:31-32	33
18:32	338, 1063, 1068
23:48	88
24:14	116
24:15-17	377
25:1-5, 10	860
33:13	323
33:14-16	326
33:17-20	326
34:2	791
35:5-6	946
36:18	947
36:26	1063
36:27	337, 1063

EZRA	Page
8:16	200

Bible Verse Cross Reference

GALATIANS	Page
1:3	256, 259, 276
1:6-9	124
1:19	123
2:4	800
2:16	626
2:17	396
2:20	396, 474
3:10	625, 628
3:15-29	635-638
3:20	74, 640
4:4-6	256, 271, 276
4:6-7	775
5:16-19	424
5:19-21	96, 518, 807, 836
5:21	88
5:22	96
5:24-25	796
6:1	796
6:7	442
6:15	306, 1050

GENESIS	Page
1:26-27	732
1:27	808, 847
1:29	543
1:31	463, 479
2:17	463
2:18	822
2:21-23	846
2:24-25	837
2:25	780
3:8-9	67
4:1	741
4:4-7	749
4:7	750, 751, 760

Copyright 2005 Edward G. Palmer, All Rights Reserved.

Book of Edward—Appendix I

Bible Verse Cross Reference

4:10	732
5:2	847
5:23-24	286
6:3	438, 471
6:4	262
6:13	466
7:1	466
8:21	697
9:1	731, 734, 822
9:4-7	731
9:5	732
9:5-6	714, 732
9:6	733, 737
9:7	731, 734
12:1	59
16:12	378
17:20	378
17:21	841
18:11	826
18:14	841
19	728
19:32	749, 860
19:36-38	860
23:1	841
25:1-2	841
25:24-26	746
28:20-22	59
29:31	711, 724
30:1-2	725
30:22	711
31:38	746
33:5	742
35:18	420
38:9	725
38:10	726
38:28-29	746
45:4-5	690

Book of Edward—Appendix I

Bible Verse Cross Reference

50:20	378
HABAKKUK	Page
1:4	966
2:15	791, 794
HEBREWS	Page
1:1-8	262
1:3	256, 276
1:3-8	261, 276
1:6	281
1:8	256, 276, 282
1:8-9	264, 265
2:17	242, 291, 464, 1052
3:1	121-123, 126
4:13	673, 780
5:9	635
5:12	143
5:13	397
6:6	143
7:21	242, 1052
8:10	76
8:11	197
9:8	649
9:10	664
9:22	468
9:27	279, 439, 509
10	1058
10:10-15	256, 274
10:18-22	827
10:19	649
10:24-25	656
10:26	40, 41, 62, 99, 305, 320, 459, 468, 486, 495, 753, 1058
10:26-31	8
10:28-31	64

Book of Edward—Appendix I

Bible Verse Cross Reference

10:29	796
11:5	286
11:6	656, 659, 775
12:2	1053
12:28	1031
13:4	831, 836, 843
13:8	133, 1064

HOSEA	Page
4:6	492
4:14	845
6:6	624
9:14	746

ISAIAH	Page
1:18	11, 21, 454, 1049
11:2	303, 304
26:3	75, 496, 1073
26:12	416
30:1	791
32:6	88
43:25	54
43:26	55
44:24	353, 711
45:9	791
49:15	711
53:4-5	519
55:9	198, 361
57:15	416
58:1	58
59:14-15	966
61:8	745

Copyright 2005 Edward G. Palmer, All Rights Reserved.

Book of Edward—Appendix I

Bible Verse Cross Reference

JAMES	Page
1:2	500
1:5	197
1:6-8	163, 197
1:17	113, 521
1:19-20	454
1:21-25	998
1:22	305, 1050
1:22-25	701
1:27	924
2:13	740
2:14-22	998
2:19	6
2:20	1061
2:23	1049
2:25-26	87, 421
3:2	142
3:7	21
3:16	295
3:17	11, 310, 454, 568
4:3	363
4:4	11, 418, 630
4:7-8	364
4:8	1058
4:17	120, 121, 328, 641, 788, 790, 791
5:11	501
5:14-15	531
5:16	356, 531

JEREMIAH	Page
1:5	746, 747
3:10	72
8:6	376
10:23	75
11:20	428
17:10	336, 428

Copyright 2005 Edward G. Palmer, All Rights Reserved.

Book of Edward—Appendix I

Bible Verse Cross Reference

18:8	114
18:10	115
20:12	428
20:18	746
22:3	946
23:1	791
23:1-4	600
23:10	865
26:3	115
26:13	115
26:13-15	946
28:15	347
29:11	521
29:11-13	177
29:13	1058
31:27	1062
31:30	1062
31:31	1062
31:31-34	251
31:33	76
31:33-34	1062
31:34	1079
32:32-35	735
42:10	115
44:22	865
49:1-6	860

JOB	Page
1:1	168, 187
1:10	524
1:21	746
1:21-22	169
3:11	747
7:15	420
12:12	200, 756
12:24	200

Book of Edward—Appendix I

Bible Verse Cross Reference

17:4	200
18:2	200
21:10	746
26:12	200
28:20-28	199
28:28	171, 756, 775
28:36	201
31:4	1074
31:15	353, 711
32:8	200
34:10	200
35:13-14	897
36:12	492
37:24	891
38:36	200, 428, 757
42:6	37

JOEL	Page
2:32	394, 406, 407, 414

JOHN	Page
1:1	256, 260, 276
1:1-3	1054
1:3	1054
1:18	261, 276
1:47	230
3:5	1029
3:9	1057
3:16	292, 315, 405, 408, 414, 1057, 1080
3:20	597
4:23	305, 1049
4:23-24	126, 228, 273, 576, 1013, 1053
4:24	281
5:6	527
5:14	43
5:19	372

Bible Verse Cross Reference

5:20	195, 1053
5:21	1004
5:22	1004
5:23	436
5:24	409, 414, 422, 475, 1003, 1006, 1008, 1010, 1056
5:24-27	158
5:26	382, 414, 1056
5:26-27	372, 1004
5:30	357
6:44	24, 250, 374, 475, 1002, 1006, 1008, 1011
6:45	250, 373, 475, 1002, 1005, 1006
6:63	242, 293
7:4	547
7:17	270, 305, 1049
7:24	149, 357, 598
7:28	195, 1053
8:11	43, 1058
8:12	162, 480
8:15-16	357
8:27	306, 1054
8:28	127, 306, 1053
8:31-32	119, 218
8:34-36	39, 135
8:34-35	775, 839
8:38	1054
8:47	415
8:52	1058
8:55	195, 251, 306, 1053
9:1-3	533
9:4	127, 195, 306, 1053
9:16	652
9:35-38	281
10:10	491
10:28	282
10:29	245, 249, 1053
10:30	293, 294, 1055

Copyright 2005 Edward G. Palmer, All Rights Reserved.

Book of Edward—Appendix I

Bible Verse Cross Reference

10:32	204, 268
11:40	205
11:41	205
12:44	249, 405, 406, 408, 1002, 1053
12:45	249
12:46	162
12:48	1002, 1006, 1008, 1010
12:50	634
13:16	195, 1052
13:36	1079
14:1	1053
14:2	285, 1079
14:3-4	285, 1079
14:6-7	388, 404, 1055, 1056
14:10	242
14:12	418, 631
14:13	1053
14:15	305, 631, 1049, 1059, 1060
14:15-23	256, 268, 276
14:16	468
14:17	304
14:20	146, 297, 1055
14:21	633
14:23	297, 474, 633, 1055, 1059
14:26	195, 468
14:28	245, 249, 306, 513, 1053, 1080
15:13	729
15:14	634, 1060
15:17	634
15:22-23	311, 461, 468, 476, 1068
15:26	256, 269, 469, 1063
16:2	379, 678
16:13	306, 1050
16:13-15	256, 269, 276
16:21	738
16:23	305, 1049
16:23-24	648, 1013

Book of Edward—Appendix I

Bible Verse Cross Reference

16:26-28	1014
17:8	242, 248, 290
17:15	524
17:23	100, 146, 777, 1055
17:26	490
19:26-27	727
20:17	196, 245, 249, 306, 1003, 1053
20:20	414
20:21	121, 122
21:17	590

1 John	Page
1:3	655
1:5	487
1:6	72, 88
1:7	486
1:9	45, 154, 357
1:10	103
2:1	305, 486, 1050
2:2	485
2:3-6	487
2:6	305, 1050
2:22	484
2:27	26, 119, 195
2:29	150, 305, 1050
3:3	305, 924, 1050
3:3-10	45
3:7	150, 306, 495, 1052
3:9	77
3:9-10	101, 104, 481
3:10	72, 88, 545, 1057
4:2-3	307, 484
4:4	1061
4:15	196
4:18	306, 1051
5:1-2	275, 276, 305, 1049

Book of Edward—Appendix I

Bible Verse Cross Reference

5:1-12	256
5:3	305, 306, 1049, 1051
5:4	128, 1061
5:5	128, 196, 306, 307, 484
5:14-15	530
5:16	279, 819
5:16-17	516
5:18	305, 1049
5:20	171, 202, 305, 415, 481, 1003, 1010, 1049, 1074

2 John	Page
1:1	26
1:7	466

3 John	Page
1:1	26
1:9-10	596

Jonah	Page
3:9	116

Joshua	Page
2:1-24	85-87
6:17	191
6:18	190, 192
10:13	264
24:15	138

Jude	Page
1:1	26, 123
1:4	770, 800, 807, 810, 839

Copyright 2005 Edward G. Palmer, All Rights Reserved.

Book of Edward—Appendix I

Bible Verse Cross Reference

JUDGES	Page
3:12-30	861
6:39-40	299
16:1	845
16:20	52
19:1	862, 863
19:2	863
19:22	749, 862
19:22-28	863
19:23-25	863
20:6	769
20:13	49, 1050
21	863

1 KINGS	Page
2:1-4	941, 973
3	738
3:11	171
3:26	737
11:2	949
11:4-11	861
12:22	264
18:37-38	341

2 KINGS	Page
2:19	746
2:21	746
17-20	742
20:1	342
20:1-6	511

LEVITICUS	Page
4:2	44, 305, 1050
4:13	44
5:17	44, 305, 1050

Copyright 2005 Edward G. Palmer, All Rights Reserved.

Book of Edward—Appendix I

Bible Verse Cross Reference

15:16-18	826
15:19	827
16:31	650
17:14	713
18:6-19	780-782
18:21	734
18:22	226, 455, 817, 839, 1059
19:15	960
19:17	348, 694, 788, 790
19:17-19	348
19:26	88
20:11	782
20:13	645, 817, 839, 1059
20:17	782
20:18	782
20:26	1066
23:34	650
23:39	650
24:5-9	650
25:2	650
26:14-17	947
27:30-33	662, 667

LUKE	Page
1:5-6	187, 306, 459
1:6	306, 1051
1:38	59
1:39-44	747
1:44	712
2:47	202
4:16	653
4:43	306, 1028, 1052
5:32	1056
6:35	362
6:37	598
6:40	100

Copyright 2005 Edward G. Palmer, All Rights Reserved.

Book of Edward—Appendix I

Bible Verse Cross Reference

6:46	27, 394, 414, 891, 1058
8:16	809
8:17	547
8:21	300
8:50	517, 519
9:60	1028
9:62	1028
10:1	123, 124
10:19	519
10:25-28	129
10:41	501
11:2-4	305, 312, 526, 1049
11:11	204, 229
11:44	1018
12:12	195, 965
12:20	510
12:32	1028
12:58	279
13:1-5	51, 52
13:3	28, 1051
13:6-9	51, 52
15:1-7	53
15:7	139
15:8-10	53
15:31-32	53, 54
16:10-12	940
16:12	673
16:13	775
16:16	1028, 1052
17:3-4	55
17:4	1065
17:20	1028
17:20-21	305, 1050
17:21	76, 1029
18:1	538
18:8	999, 1015
18:29-30	1029

Book of Edward—Appendix I

Bible Verse Cross Reference

19:46	ix, 546
20:9-19	1057
20:35-36	492
21:31	1029
22:35	492
22:50-51	346
23:43	282, 283
24:45	203, 415

2 MACCABEES	Page
12:43-46	279

4 MACCABEES	Page
1:1-6	220
1:3-4	967
1:6	967
1:15-20	220
1:18	967
1:28-35	221
1:35-2:4	895
2:1-3:18	233
2:10	755
2:10-13	238
2:11	755
2:12	755
2:13	755
5:22-24	967

MALACHI	Page
1:6	1064
2:2	865, 1060
2:7-8	455, 582, 591, 1065
2:10	1064
2:15	316, 923
2:16	745

Copyright 2005 Edward G. Palmer, All Rights Reserved.

Book of Edward—Appendix I

Bible Verse Cross Reference

2:17	455, 1065
3	667
3:5	417, 645
3:6	101, 133, 290, 1064
3:8-10	584, 629, 665
3:8-12	665, 667
3:11	746
3:16	584
3:16-17	665
4:2	519

MARK	Page
1:4	1046
1:11	211
1:15	1027
4:11	452
6:2	194
6:8-13	16
7:7	ix, 1060
7:15	141
7:20-23	141, 155, 807
7:21-23	696, 697, 768
9:23	449
9:47	1027
10:14	1059
10:18	295, 1053
10:52	519, 530
11:24	312
12:1-12	1057
12:26-27	286
12:29	1063
12:30	305, 1049
12:32	305, 306, 1049
12:42-44	672
13:32	1052
14:36	538

Bible Verse Cross Reference

14:58	18
16:17-18	12, 519, 552
16:20	12

MATTHEW	Page
1:1-17	722
2:2	281
2:11	281
3:1-2	460
3:2	28
3:5-6	460
3:8	47, 1066
3:16	256, 266, 276
3:17	256, 267, 276
4:4	590
4:10	126, 305, 1013, 1049
4:17	28, 125, 306, 459, 1019, 1052
5:3	1019
5:7	740
5:8	162, 924
5:10	1019
5:13	471
5:17	582
5:17-18	1064, 1065
5:18-20	789
5:19	194, 632, 1051
5:20	4, 5, 107, 163, 414, 1019, 1060
5:25	279
5:28	765
5:29	1060, 1061
5:30	843, 844
5:48	100, 777
6:5-7	312
6:6	280, 306, 1050
6:10	1019
6:13	1019

Copyright 2005 Edward G. Palmer, All Rights Reserved.

Book of Edward—Appendix I

Bible Verse Cross Reference

6:14	1050
6:20	141
6:24	1067
6:31-34	941
6:33	1019
7	150, 990, 996, 997
7:1	356
7:13-14	150, 305, 1015
7:14	453, 1014
7:15	800
7:16	10, 597
7:21	989, 1020
7:21-23	Cover, 3, 38, 50, 80, 83, 332, 395, 623, 1007, 1040, 1056, 1059
7:22	107, 108
7:22-23	ix, 14, 20, 996
7:23	4, 88, 98, 244, 996
7:24	997
7:26	997
8:10-11	1020
8:12	1020
8:17	519
8:20	661
9:13	459, 624
9:22	530
9:29	530
9:35	1020
10:1	124
10:2	123
10:7	1020
10:8	124
10:19-20	534
10:28	306, 420, 686, 692, 1050, 1051, 1062, 1078
10:34-36	579
11:4-5	533
11:11	1021
11:12	989, 1021

Copyright 2005 Edward G. Palmer, All Rights Reserved.

Book of Edward—Appendix I

Bible Verse Cross Reference

11:20	28
11:29	500
12:2	652
12:6-7	652
12:7	740
12:8	652
12:12	653
12:25	950, 1021
12:31	375
12:32	279
12:35	362
12:50	891, 1053
13:8	629
13:11	1021
13:19	1021
13:24-25	1022
13:31	1022
13:33	1022
13:37-43	1023
13:41	632
13:43	414
13:44	1023
13:45-46	1023
13:47-50	1023
13:52	1024
13:55-58	526, 527
14:33	281
15:1-2	13
15:3	244, 1042
15:3-6	14
15:6	457
15:7-9	1017
15:8-9	ix
15:9	395, 1060
15:14	1042
15:16-20	142
16:3	1017

Bible Verse Cross Reference

15:28	530
16:19	989, 1024
16:23	573
16:26	673
16:27	1061
16:28	1024
17:5	207
17:24-27	661
18:3-4	1024
18:6	334, 1059
18:6-7	788, 790, 797, 805
18:8-9	504
18:10	1059
18:14	1059
18:15-17	47
18:18-19	519
18:21-22	56
18:23	1024
18:35	1024
19:4	847
19:4-6	296
19:5	1055
19:5-6	847
19:6	837
19:8-9	923
19:12	1025
19:14	1025, 1059
19:16-19	306, 1051
19:16-24	80
19:17	458
19:17-18	632
19:17-20	129, 414
19:21	777
19:23	457
19:23-24	1025
19:30	892
20:1	1025

Book of Edward—Appendix I

Bible Verse Cross Reference

20:14-16	1025
21:12-13	581, 582
21:28-32	679, 682
21:31	1026
21:33-42	1057
21:43	1026
22:2	1026
22:29	173, 1063
22:31-32	1018
22:37-40	244, 633
22:40	306, 414, 632, 1051
23:1-2	1065
23:1-5	562
23:3-4	152
23:13	563, 1017, 1026
23:14	791, 1017
23:15	545, 1017
23:23	616, 618, 620, 625, 639, 740, 1017, 1065
23:25	1017
23:28	545, 800
24	999, 1006
24:6	940
24:14	1026, 1052
24:36	252, 1052
24:37-39	999
24:40-42	999
24:46	1000
24:50-51	1000
25	985, 990, 992, 994, 996, 999, 1006, 1007
25:1	999, 1027
25:1-13	977, 992
25:14	1027
25:14-30	993
25:31-40	994
25:32-34	977
25:34	1027
25:35-46	624

Copyright 2005 Edward G. Palmer, All Rights Reserved.

Book of Edward—Appendix I

Bible Verse Cross Reference

25:44	995
25:45	995
25:46	1006, 1007, 1008, 1011
26:29	1027
26:39	292
27:46	290
28:9	281
28:19	256, 267
28:19-20	15, 124, 276
28:20	1060

MICAH	Page
2:1	88

NUMBERS	Page
12:12	746
14:9	943
15:33-36	650
18:21-26	668
23:19	28, 113, 290
25:4-5	344
25:6-11	345
35:22-24	349
35:30-32	350
35:33-34	349

1 PETER	Page
1:2	25, 256, 274, 276
1:15	1066
1:15-17	50
2:9	18
2:24	358, 519
3:12	10, 150, 1011, 1056
3:18-20	279
4:3	807

Copyright 2005 Edward G. Palmer, All Rights Reserved.

Book of Edward—Appendix I

Bible Verse Cross Reference

4:14	304
4:17	635
4:19	440
5:7	500

2 Peter	Page
1:1	25
2:15	134
2:16	134
2:14-22	135
2:18	810, 839
2:19	134
2:20	495

Philippians	Page
1:7	124
1:17	124
1:29	439
2:2	926
2:12	893
2:15	204
3:3	256, 273, 276, 281
3:10	629
3:19	926
3:21	629
4:8	155, 786
4:19	240

Proverbs	Page
1:7	897
3:5	198, 1073
3:12	747
3:16-17	544
3:33	864
4:23	753, 754

Copyright 2005 Edward G. Palmer, All Rights Reserved.

Bible Verse Cross Reference

5:18-19	821
5:23	492
6:16	745
8:13	692
10:12	229, 1078
11:31	1016
12:2	362
12:26	139
14:12	393
14:26	496
16:2	336, 350, 924
16:8	897
17:26	966
18:24	1049
19:22	897
20:11	924
21:2	702
22:14	749, 774, 841
23:7	765
24:25	864
28:6	899
28:13	591
30:6	966
30:12	924

PSALM	Page
1	891
1:1-6	166
1:5	445, 891
1:6	891, 1062
3:8	382, 414
4:3	891
5:5	745
5:6	745
9:1	72
11:5	379

Copyright 2005 Edward G. Palmer, All Rights Reserved.

Book of Edward—Appendix I

Bible Verse Cross Reference

Reference	Page
12:6-7	924
16:11	75
18:2	382
18:32	416
18:46	382
19:7-8	627
19:8-9	924
22:3	18
22:10	742
23:3	686
25:14	692
27:1	382
27:5-6	500
31:14-15	172, 376, 1074
33:18	692
34:10	492, 496
34:17	519
34:17-19	498
34:18	1073
34:21	897
37:23	362
37:39	382
45:7	745
46:10	251
50:16-21	545
50:23	382, 414
51:1-13	36
51:14-17	37
72:14	714
82:6-7	269
91:11	524
91:16	438
97:10	745
103:13	692, 739
103:15-16	173
107:20	519
111:1	72

Copyright 2005 Edward G. Palmer, All Rights Reserved.

Book of Edward—Appendix I

Bible Verse Cross Reference

111:10	202, 692, 1051
116:4	280
118:5	519
119:2	72
119:10	72
119:30-32	437
119:35	416
119:104	171, 745
119:105	416, 451
119:113	745
127:3	742
135:14	114
139:13	353
139:13-15	747
139:13-16	712, 742
139:14-18	1059
139:21	745
139:23-24	416
141:4	88
143:2	626
145:9	739
146:9	614

REVELATIONS	Page
1-3	1054, 1058
1:1	26
1:4-7	287, 288
1:4-8	302
1:8	287, 288
1:10-11	288
1:13-16	288
2:4-5	587
2:6	133, 134, 1064
2:10	170, 440, 941
2:14	134
2:15	134, 1064

Copyright 2005 Edward G. Palmer, All Rights Reserved.

Book of Edward—Appendix I

Bible Verse Cross Reference

Verse	References
2:19-21	1005
3	1054, 1058
3:1	303, 1064
3:4	228
3:4-5	586
3:12	242, 365, 1052, 1053
3:14	242, 260, 262, 306, 1053, 1054
3:15-16	165
3:16	384
4:5	303
4:8	288
4:16	34
5:3	279
5:4-9	263
5:6	265, 303
5:7	288
5:13	279, 1053
7:10	157, 372, 382, 414, 1004, 1056
9:20	204
10:7	452
11:15	308
11:16-18	288
17:13	926
19:10	281
21:1	1018
21:4	1018
21:5-6	288
21:8	644, 749, 755, 792, 793, 797, 839, 848, 956
21:27	897, 957
22:1	893
22:6-7	288
22:11	97, 175, 1066
22:12	1062
22:12-13	288
22:13	256, 266, 276
22:14	77, 645, 676
22:15	38, 77, 84, 88, 645, 676, 749, 755, 839, 848,

Bible Verse Cross Reference

	897, 957, 991, 1059
22:18-19	152, 193

ROMANS	Page
1-2	809, 810, 1059
1:4	304
1:7	256, 258, 276
1:8	25
1:18	38, 644, 991
1:18-32	88
1:20	461
1:24-27	1060
1:24-29	850
1:25	226
1:26	226, 817, 839, 843, 844, 850
1:27	839, 843, 844
1:28-32	810, 839
1:29	226
1:30-31	851
1:32	149, 1059
2:2-3	811, 839
2:5-11	69
2:7-24	68
2:12	306, 1051
2:14-15	753
2:15	76
2:21	59
2:23	1065
2:29	59, 306, 630, 1050
3:8	350
4:3	187
4:8	396, 414
4:17	537
6:1	1057
6:1-2	333
6:3	556

Bible Verse Cross Reference

6:4	1047
6:6-7	333
6:10	41
6:16	1060
6:16-18	305, 1050
6:18	398
6:18-20	776
6:22	398, 414
6:23	413, 1051
7:19	101, 103, 105
7:21-23	776
8:1	305, 423, 1050
8:5	423
8:8-10	74
8:9	73, 423
8:11	519
8:13-14	73
8:28	521
9:1	73
9:15	381, 492
9:20-21	381
9:21	809
10:2-3	351
10:8-10	5
10:9-10	389, 397, 1048, 1068
10:10	414
10:13	5, 394, 407
10:17	2, 583
11:5	228
12:1	878
12:2	629, 925
12:3	950
12:9	508, 743
12:16	925
12:17	351
13	306, 1050
13:3	598, 953

Copyright 2005 Edward G. Palmer, All Rights Reserved.

Book of Edward—Appendix I

Bible Verse Cross Reference

13:10	678, 1065
13:13	768, 807
14:17	1030
15:5-6	926
15:17-20	124
16:7	123

1 SAMUEL	Page
14	861
15:29	114

2 SAMUEL	Page
11	727
12:21-33	376, 492, 526
22:37	416
22:26-28	924

SONG OF SOLOMON	Page
4:5	828
4:16	828
5:1	828

SIRACH	Page
16:14	740
17:25-26	36
17:26	745
18:9-14	34
18:13	739
28:4	740
32:14-17	236
33:14	29
38:1-8	515
38:16-21	1080
38:16-23	514

Copyright 2005 Edward G. Palmer, All Rights Reserved.

Book of Edward—Appendix I

Bible Verse Cross Reference

SUSANNA	Page
1:9	966

1 THESSALONIANS	Page
1:1	123
2:4	336
2:12	1030
5:23	419

2 THESSALONIANS	Page
1:3	2
1:5	1031
1:6	351
2:7	452
2:9-12	x, 225, 578, 1067
2:10	685, 748, 896, 1038, 1051
2:11-12	677, 748
3:10	912

1 TIMOTHY	Page
1:5	162
1:7	775
1:9-10	642
1:19	154
1:20	597
2:5	22, 648
2:8	554
3:9	163
3:16	452
4:16	416
5:3-4	906
5:8	15
5:19-20	592
6:3-5	589

Book of Edward—Appendix I

Bible Verse Cross Reference

2 Timothy	Page
1:7	172, 775
2:15	95
2:17-18	597
2:19	97, 120
2:19-21	809
2:22	163
3:1-7	741
3:3	770
3:16	95, 1063
3:16-17	676
4:2	582
4:3-4	ix, x, 227, 578, 1067
4:11	123
4:14	597
4:18	1031

Titus	Page
1:4	123
1:5	613
1:9-11	613
1:15	163
1:16	613
3:4-7	474, 491
3:5-6	337

Wisdom	Page
1:8	967
1:11	897, 956
14:22-31	968

Zechariah	Page
5:4	865
7:9	740
8:17	745

Copyright 2005 Edward G. Palmer, All Rights Reserved.

Book of Edward—Appendix I

Bible Verse Cross Reference

12:10	303, 304
13:9	280

ZEPHANIAH	Page
2:8	860

OTHER ANCIENT MANUSCRIPTS DISCUSSED	Page
APOCRYPHON OF JAMES	478
BOOK OF THOMAS	479

ENOCH

48:7	1081
50:2	1081
69:12	736
68:18	736
81:4	1081

GOSPEL OF MARY	479
GOSPEL OF PHILIP	479, 480, 504, 505

GOSPEL OF THOMAS

#70, #99	478

GOSPEL OF TRUTH	479

SURAH OF QURAN

5:116-117	1012

SECRET BOOK OF JOHN	479

Book of Edward

Appendix J
Index

It's February 1, 2005 and almost four years since I wrote the first chapter. I've just finished indexing the book. The Appendixes are not indexed except for a few items. God's Spirit has been with me these last weeks as I indexed what HE guided my spirit to index for you. Therefore, this is not a concordance where you will find all instances or citations of any given word. It is simply an Index of spiritual topics for you to consider. You will get the most of the book reading it front to back. And, you will encounter all instances of any given topic by doing so. Yet with the Appendixes provided, including this Index, you will be able to enhance and maximize your search for the truth of God's Word.

PRAYER: "Merciful Almighty God of Heaven, bless all who read and study from this 'Book of Edward' that they may renew a commitment to YOU and be found worthy to enter into YOUR kingdom. The 'kingdom message' was Christ's Gospel that YOU gave him to preach. Indeed, Christ's human sacrifice was confirmation to the world that another life exists that is more glorious than this fleshly life. It is YOUR kingdom that awaits YOUR people. Therefore, open up understanding and give Christ's 'gospel of the kingdom message' to the hearts of all who open up the pages of this book in search for YOUR truth. O' LORD, let this work of YOUR Spirit save many souls. In Christ's precious name, as his brother, I plead for mercy on all the nations and all of humanity and ask this of you FATHER." The Apostle Edward

Study Note: Left column is read top to bottom. It then continues on top of the adjacent right hand column. The bottom of the right hand column then continues at the top of the left column on following page.

Index

9/11, 94
Abhor, 37
Abhorred, by God, 749
Abide, 119
Abominations
  List of seven, 374
Abortion, 35
  1,500,000 Babies per year, 698
  11 oz Premature baby lives, 738
  A time to hate, 743
  Abomination to God, 679
  AbortionFacts.com, 709
  AbortionTV.com, 709
  Act of selfishness, ungodly love, 729
  Adoption in 1960's, 703
  An incredible evil, 735
  Bible speaks against, 353, 678
  Blood belongs to soul, 732
  Blood cries out from ground, 732
  Body parts market, 681
  Children are a gift from God, 742
  Choice is murder, 701
  Christ's genealogy, 723
  Coat hangers, 703
  Compassion, 719
  Complications, 705
  Doctor, 339
  Eclipse of Reason, 704
  Egg selection process, 713
  Embryonic stem cells, 730
  Execution of Paul J. Hill, 340
  Exodus 21 exegesis, 745
  Fallen Angel teaches man, 736
  Fertilized eggs, 339
  Fetal development facts, 705
  Framed in love language, 691
  Future descendants, genocide, 718
  God says to choose life, 724
  God speaks, 347
  God speaks, life in blood, 713
  God supports, mythology, 748
  God's instructions to nurture, 712
  God's perspectives, three, 691
  God's Word prohibits, 733
  Hate what God hates, 693
  Heart v. Intellect, 680
  If you've had one, 747
  Incest, 722
  Incest discussion, Christ, 725
  Industry, 681
  Kills more Democrats, 688
  Legal full nine months, 704
  Life belongs to God, 731
  Life exists in womb, 715
  Life of mother, specious, 729
  Lifestyle choice, 719
  Love does no wrong, 678
  Lucky sperm? 712
  Mary, act of love for God, 727
  Mind v. Heart graphic, 695
  Miracle of Life, Nova special, 711
  Miscarriage, natural form, 704
  Murder, 339
  Neonatology, 716
  Nine characteristics of love, 683
  No Constitutional right, 698
  No unwanted child, specious, 703
  Not option for God's people, 347
  Partial birth, 703
  Perspective on love, 737
  Pregnancy myth, 704
  Pre-Roe stigma removed, 698
  Rape, 721
  Rationalized by man, 679
  Response from God, 946
  Right to life, U.S. Founders, 700
  Right to murder, Kerry, 702
  Sacrifice of offspring, forbidden, 734
  Selective reduction, 720
  Support, repenting to God, 747
  Surgery in womb, 717
  Teens, murder in eyes of law, 704
  Test, would you abort? 709
  To understand, heart for God, 681

Index

Abortion (Continued)
    Ultrasound images, 710
    v. God's help in procreation, 741
    v. Mercy, 740
    v. Mother's joy, 738
    v. Opened heart, 727
    v. Poverty, 739
    Value of baby, 683
    Viable human debate specious, 715
    Warning, 748
    Willing womb, baby lives, 715
    Womb protects life, 711
    Women's right to know truth, 708
    See Womb
Abortionites, 741
Abraham
    Discussion of religions, 367
    Father of three religions graphic, 366
    Uprooted family for God, 65
Absent From Body, 422
Abundantly, 7
    God's Spirit poured out, 337
Abuse, Spiritual
    Subtle Power of Spiritual Abuse by authors David Johnson and Jeff VanVonderen, 617
Accomplished, 416
Accursed
    Definition, 191
Action, 758
    God's perspective, 691
Adams, John, 950
Adams, John Quincy, 952
Adulterers, 38
Adultery, 402
Adventure, 57
    B. Dalton Bookstore, graphic, 208
AFCM, 560
Aggressive
    Salvation workers, 97
Alcoholics Anonymous, 32
Alien, 417

Alpha & Omega
    See Trinity Doctrine
Amish, 1015
Amused, 22
Amy, vii, 525
Anarchy
    Is no discrimination, 986
Angels, Like, 492
Anglicans, 370
Anointed
    Book of Edward, 2
    Siding with the Pastor? 579
Anointed (singing group)
    The Word (song), 1040
Anointing, 17, 119
    Real, 27
Answers
    Come from understanding, 177
    Get them from Jesus, 214
Antichrist
    Claims Christ is God, 307
    Speaks against humanity of Son, 307
Anxiety, 61
Apocryphal Books
    Deleted circa 1300, 234
    Discussion, 479
Apocryphon of James, 478
Apocryphon of John, 479
Apostasy
    Rationalization, 130
    Subtle, 567
    See Nicolaitans
Apostle
    Commissioned by God, 110
    Definition, 121, 122
    Edward's authority, 125
    Edward's reluctance, 125
    Heart of, 94
    Jesus Christ, 104, 122
    List of ninety-six in Bible, 123
    List of twelve things they do, 124
    Messenger of God, 124
    Planted, 602

Index

Apostle (Continued)
    Respects Christ's words, 105
    Trusts God, 102
    Without money, 492
Apostles
    False, 595
    Identified evildoers, 597
Appointed, 509
Appointed Time, 422
Apricot Seeds, 540
Archie (Jackie's dad), 529, 537
    Incubated on oven door, 717
Armor, 525, 531
Artificial Life Machines, 506
    Insurance, 507
    When to pull plug, 507
Ask, 363
Astonishing, 4
    50% factor, 9, 977
Astray, Led, 614, 619
Awaken
    Christians, 2
    Jews, 2
    Muslims, 2
B.I.B.L.E, 975
Babies
    Unskilled in righteousness, 397
Baby Milk, 396
Badgering, 110
Balance Scale, 1009
Ban
    Evildoers from Church, 359
Baptism
    Doctrine, 1046
Baptized, 556
Barb, vii, 535, 727
Beat
    Sinners into submission, 97
Begotten
    Human Son, 7, 292
Behavior
    Crowd doesn't hide yours, 797
    Error prone, 101
    Has consequences with God, 1038
    Old v. New, 30
Belief
    Demonstration of, 639
    In God v. Jesus, 1003
    In heart, 5
    Moved from head to heart, 6
    Sincere, 701
    Steadfast, 632
    Unto righteousness, 5
    See Righteousness
Belief, In Son, 248
Belief, True, 397
Believer
    Encourage one another, 656
    Hallmark traits, 29
    Insincere giveaway, 29
    Join small group, need, 655
Beloved
    Those called, 26
Belshazzar, 89
    Lesson in obedience, 92
    Son of Nebuchadnezzar, 90
Benjamin, vii
Bereans
    Searched Scripture, 94
Bernice (Jackie's aunt), 505, 508
Bestiality, 814
Bezaleel, 171
Bible
    B.I.B.L.E., 23
    Book about Yahweh, 490
    Chronological, 216
    Computer software, 216
    Cross Reference of Verses, 1134
    Deserves universal attention, 952
    Discussion of modern tools, 217
    Don't read it message, 206
    Ignorance no excuse, 248
    Ignorant Christians, 95
    Infallible? 94
    Job 38:36 translation, 757
    Letters to you? 680

Index

Bible (Continued)
  Lost books of, 264
  Mosaic from God, 128
  Not about Jesus, 247
  Not taught in church, 583
  Parallel, 216
  Plain and simple language, 188
  Reasons to trust, 23
  Red lettered, 213
  Reinterpretations, 369
  Religions, leave it at home, 549
  Speaks against abortion, 353
  Stands on two laws, 633
  Storybook, not a, 562
  Written for Christians, 681
Bible Commentaries
  Promote mythology, 255
Bible Study Group, 583
Bible Study Leader
  Commissioned by God, 110
Bible Translation
  Truth v. translation, 119
Bible Translation Debate, 119
Bible Translations
  Bible Identifier, 3-4 Caps, iii
  List of Bibles referenced, iii
  Nuances, but ~99% in agreement, 133
  Twenty-five cited in book, iii
Bible, Believing
  Choice from heart, 167
Bibles
  Colorful notes, 599
  Customized apostate trend, 112
  Gender neutralization, 112
Biblical Integrity
  Accuracy of Edward, ii
  Original translation referenced, ii
  Presented text, ii
Birth Control, 856
Bishops, Episcopal, 319, 334, 351, 368, 375
  Blaspheme, 369
  Headed to hell, 455

Bitterness
  Not opposite of forgiveness, 54
  See Forgiveness
Blameless, 571
Blasphemy, 100
    Ultimate, 774
    Unforgiven, type, 375
Blessed, 501
Blood
  Belongs to soul, 732
  Result of shedding innocent, 946
Blood, Covenant
  Trampled on, 64
Blot Out Sins, 54
Blue In Face, 399
Blume, Judy
  Are You There God? It's Me, Margaret, 799
Body
  Without spirit is dead, 421
Body, Stressed, 497
Bold, 3
Book of Thomas, 217, 479
Books, Holy
  Sequence of three, 370
Born in Vain, 1037
Born of God, 77
  Does not sin, 45
Branch Dividian, 368
Breastfeeding, 855
Brian, vii, 229, 839
  Born, 856
Bristol, Claude M
  Magic of Believing, 198
Broken Spirit
  Sacrifice of, 37
Budwig, Johanna Dr, 543
Burden, 499
Burdensome
  Commandments are not, 1051
Bush, George W, 778, 898, 901
Cadillac
  Gift example, 7

Index

Calls
   His name, 5
Calm
   Reason to be, 63
Cancer, 492, 518
   12 Things to consider, 541
   Apricots, B17, 540
   Budwig Diet, 543
   Killing protocols, 1083
   Laetrile, 542
Cancer, Pancreatic, 503, 539
Capitalization Protocol of Book
   God shown by "Lord," ii
   God shown by small caps, ii
   Jesus shown by "Lord," ii
   Jesus shown by lower case, ii
   Original translation issue, ii
Carmen, Eric (song), 879
CBS News, 956
Cells, Body, 520
Ceremonies
   Major religions, 679
Change
   Dramatic, 30
Changed Man, 71
Character, 589
   God dislikes, 29
   God likes, 29
Character, God's
   Unchanging, 247
Character, Good
   Bad company corrupts, 445
Charismatic, 513
   Errant wealth teachings, 16
Cheney, Dick, 778
Child of God, 545
Chinese Grandfather, 687
Choice
   All love and sex, 866
   Each individual's, 97
   First one is ours, 316
   Graphic, we move up or down, 139
   To accept God's Word, 387
   To live in God's zones, 166
   Two separate directions, 142
Choices
   Edify or defile your life, 141
   God knows yours, 167
   Graphic, Choice for God, 144
   Graphic, Choice for Satan, 145
   Graphic, Pattern for God, 145
   Graphic, Pattern for Satan, 146
   Lead to Heaven or Hell, 140
   Righteous from heart, 170
   Six from heart we all make, 138
   Type of fruit, 132
   See Edward; Faithful; Job
Choices, Backslider
   Defined, Graphic, 156
Choices, Bold
   Defined, Graphic, 159
Choices, Conviction
   Defined, Graphic, 160
Choices, Repentant
   Defined, Graphic, 157
Choices, Wide Path
   Defined, Graphic, 161
Choose
   Blessings over curses, 132
   God's Word or Pastor's, 187
   Life over death, 132
Christ, A Crisis in the Life of God, 210
Christ's Spirit
   Inside you, 147
Christian
   Best definition, 7
   Confused, 495
   Defined by Edward, 371
   Discernment, 800
   Duty to care, not government's, 996
   First big test, 549
   Integrity, 899
   Meaningless word, 483
   Mindset, 457
   No duty to evil government, 954
   Original meaning, 483

Index

Christian (Continued)
    Politics matter, results, 974
    Real, debate, 40
    Servants, 50% Raptured, 1000
    Three part circle graphic, 373
    Unrighteous, 495
    Voting data, 910
    Who is, 6
Christianity
    Crowd mentality, 798
    Gnostic, 476
    v. New Age dogma, 985
Christians
    50% Found wanting, 1009
    50% or more going to hell, 977
    Intellectually lazy, some, 246
    Like Pinocchio seeking money, 588
    Not a worldly focus, 630
    Programmed, 589
    Should be like minded, 926
    Silent about evil & crime, 547
    Support evil, impunity myth, 980
    Tithe programming, false, 618
    Unprepared, 997
Christopher, vii, 502, 839, 841, 893
Church
    Articles & By-laws, 674
    Biblical discrimination, 987
    Collecting souls for Satan, 393
    Dressed for Satan, 594
    Hierarchy, 21
    Hot, filled with Spirit, viii
    How it supports evil, 594
    How to steal, 602
    Hypocrites, 599
    Large, 655
    Leaving, emotional, 577
    Membership criteria, 674
    People who have left, 656
    Rules, voluntary, 653
    Sex talk, scared of, 768
    Sex teachings, source, 818
    Worldwide Harvest Church, 190
Church, Types, 560
    Bible believing v. non, graphic, 561
    Bible ignorant graphic, 584
    Counterfeit, Word of Faith, 579
    Evil rampant in churches, 1015
    Fifteen warnings, 580
    Focus of ministry, fruits, 585
    Homosexual, 810
    Hypocritical, 1017
    Individual hearts, graphic, 587
    Individual v. Church graphic, 585
    Mainline, 562
    New Testament, 610
    New Testament, defined, 613
    Pseudo acts of caring, useless, 1005
    Satan's Catch 22, 576
    Satanic, 564, 992
    Seven questions to answer, 564
    Seven signs of satanic church, 586
    Sign of Satan's church, 581
    Six Ministries of God, 565
    Spiritually abusive, 617
    Use of emotion graphic, 574
    Word of Faith, 14, 560
    Zone discussion, 575
    Zones, 562
Clarity, 631
Clinton
    Adultery & lies to Court, 772
    Contrasted to Lincoln, 760
    Idol, Kennedy, 931
    Impeachment, lies to Court, 954
    Oral sex, 236, 773
    Parsing words, 236
    Politics of destruction, 956
    Product of apostate Christianity, 491
    Selfish ambitions, 954
    Sexual fiasco, 234
    Testimony, 236
    See Lying
Cohabitation, 833
    Mortal sin, 842
Comatose, 508

Index

Comma
    Paradise statement on cross, 284
Commandments, Kept
    Elizabeth and Zacharias, 187
Commands
    To obey, 635
Commingling, 948
Commitment
    No alternatives, 32
Communications
    After Christ graphic, 647
    Before Christ graphic, 646
    Christ your mediator, 647
    Getting truth out, 568
    God wants it two-way, 649
    God's channel, graphic, 430
    God's plan, 22
    Holy of Holies, new access, 649
    Jesus says go direct to God, 648
    Men v. women, humorous, 63
    No intermediary to God, 647
    One half of the letters, 681
    Open door to God, 21
    Satan has world to, 432
    Satan's channel, graphic, 431
Community
    How it supports evil, 596
Compassion, 109, 719
    God's, 34
Compromise, 666
    None, 15
Concerns, Earthly, 501
Conclusion, 1037
Condemned
    By one's own choices, 1036
    See Friend
Confess
    God raised Jesus, 5
Confession, 5
    Coupled with righteousness, 5
    David's prayer of, 36
Confidence, 496, 498
Confirmation, 6
Congregations
    Manipulated, 95
Connie, 509, 514, 537
Conscience, Lack of, 767
Consequences, 686
Constitution, U.S.
    For moral & religious people, 952
Context
    Bible taken out of, 128
Context, Larger
    Unchanging character of God, 246
Contract
    See Law
Contrast
    Of repentant sinner, 54
Control
    Give it to God, 65
    Principle, 82
Control, Losing (moral), 880
Conundrum
    Faith v. Law, 642
Conversations With God
    Neale Donald Walsch, 980
Conversion
    Jews doubt Paul, 30
Converted, Property, 568
Conviction, Real, 160
Counseling, 32
Counterfeit, 578
    Miracles, report, 608
Covenant
    Abraham's, 635
    Individuals, 76
    Marriage, 316
Covetous, 39
Created
    Naked, sexual & holy, 780
Cross
    God's gift, 485
    Muslim belief, 476
    Not God in flesh, 128
    Pick it up daily, 102

Copyright 2005 Edward G. Palmer, All Rights Reserved.

Book of Edward—Appendix J

Index

Cross, Empty
  Discussion, 434
Crucified
  With Christ, 74
Crucifix, 433
Crucifying Christ
  Sinful lifestyle, 9
Cryptic, 250
Culprits in Pulpits, 619
Cults, Christian, 15, 150
Curse
  Living under, 660
Cursed, 625
Damascus, 33
Darwin, 985
Days, Length of, 510
De Becker, Gavin
  The Gift of Fear, 771
Dead, 492
Dean, vii, 177, 743
  Don't support evil, 805
Death
  A time to rejoice, 513
  Absence, 503
  Dignity, 506
  Graphic, 426
  Judgment v. transfer, 285
  Letting go, 537
  Lost dreams, 978
  Science trying to cheat, 509
  Sudden, 509
  You don't know when, 510
  See Remembrance
Debased, 778
Deception, 136, 606
Default Bible Used
  See New King James
Democratic Party, 10
  Absolutist moral dogma, 913
  Created a dependency class, 916
  Democrat societal changes, 969
  Lacked wisdom with Clinton, 234
  Legacy is moral turpitude, 970
  Playbook of lies, 955
  Policies with no spiritual weight, 995
  Responsible for moral decay in United States, 931
  Rights of man ideology, 931
  Soak the rich mentality, 903
  Stands for perversion, 702
  Supports abortion, 10
  Supports homosexuality, 10
Demons
  Believe, 6
Depart
  All who practice lawlessness, 3
Departed
  Spirit from Samson, 52
Descriptions
  Those called, 26
Desire
  To please God, 40
Dialogue
  Remarkable Bible, 319
Diamonds, 16
Dinking, Alcohol, 515
Discerning God's Will
  Four principles, 66
Discernment, 102, 800
Discrimination, 986
Dishonor, Vessel of, 808
Disrespect, 364
Divorce, 885, 923
Do Not Practice
  Checklist, 88
Do The Right Thing, 791
Docetism, 476
Doctrinal Statement, 1049
  KJV, NKJV & NIV Supports, 112
Doers of Word, 701
Doesn't Change
  See God & Jesus Christ
Dogma, 14, 792
Double Minded, 163
Draw Close To God
  In HIS Presence graphic, 365

Index

Drawn, To Church, 556
Dreams
   When they're broken, 979
Drug Companies, 543
Drunk
   In Holy Spirit, viii
Drunkards, 38
Duplicitous, 941
Duty
   To confront sin, 55
   See Forgetting
Duty to Care, 996
Duty, Man's, 369
Dwell
   God inside you, 16
   Not in man's structures, God, 16
   Within you, God, 8
Dylan, vii, 714
Earl, 505
Ears, Itching Christian, 575
Ecstasy
   Sexual, spiritual, 881
Eden
   Living in, 7
   Return to, 452
Education
   Evolution theory taught as fact, 985
   God filling, contrast, 175
   Truth of U.S. History hidden, 985
Edward
   A great joy, 501
   Abortion support repentance, 747
   Baptism Testimony, 555
   Call
      Observe, witness, worship, 558
      Tell them to change name, 559
   Changed life, 450, 548
   Church evolution, graphic, 560
   Doctrinal Statement, 1049
   Fined for telling truth in Court, 965
   Gift of tongues, 553
   Goodbye to Jackie, 1072
   Life history, highlights, 446
   Limit reached, 449
   Metaphysical encounter, 604
   New Scripture, 127
   Personal horror, Jackie's death, 978
   Procrastinating, 493
   Sexuality, 756
   Son of God, brother of Christ, 1004
   Spiritual influences, 438
   Spiritual milestone, 604
   Spiritual training, 551, 555
   Suffering, 514
   Taste of Job's misery, 169
   Thirst for truth, 442
   Thoughts of another wife, 868
   Water Baptism, 555
   Worse fear, 494
   Writings deceived (not), 455
Elect
   Those called, 25
Elk River Assembly of God, 546
   Edward drawn to, 556
   Growth and influence, 557
   Hoogenboom sex misconduct, 558
   Name change, 559
   Sex scandal, 557
Embittered, 54
Embodied, 29
Embryonic Stem Cells, 730
Emotions
   Reason rules, discussion, 230
End Times
   Ezra prays for mankind, 1033
   Fifteen lessons, 990
   God explains precious few, 1036
   God tells Ezra the signs, 1035
   Jesus defines wise and foolish, 997
   Jesus teaches, Matthew 7, 996
   Jesus teaches, Matthew 25, 992
   Likened to ten virgins, 50/50, 980
   Multitude perish, born in vain, 1036
   New Age Christianity, 980
   One group not judged, 1001
   Rapture has 50% factor, 999

Copyright 2005 Edward G. Palmer, All Rights Reserved.

Index

End Times (Continued)
    Signs of kingdom, 1029
    Society has upside down mores, 985
    Summary of New Age dogma, 984
    Three groups are judged, 1001
    Workers, 50% Raptured, 999
Enmity Towards God
    Friends of world, 418
Enoch, 286
Enoch, Book of, iii
Epilogue, 1039
Epiphany
    Edward's, 2, 438, 450
Episcopal
    See Bishops
Erroneous, 9
Esoteric, 19
Essence, Your Earthly
    Graphic, 427
Eternal Death
    For evildoers, 1012
Eternal Life
    By keeping commandments, 80
    Christian sorting, lawless, 1007
    Entering, Christ teaches, 504
    Few find it, 453
    For do-gooders, 1012
    God's no judgment graphic, 1008
    Jesus' judgment graphic, 1008
    Last day pick up by Jesus, 422
    Love God, 129
    Nation sorting, righteous, 1007
    Obey commandments, 129
    Those who already have it, 422, 1001
    Two Groups in heaven, graphic, 1006
    Two Groups in hell, graphic, 1006
Evil
    All sin is, 45
    Confronting, 569
    Don't turn your back on, 55
    Exposing, 567
    Google, 859
    Half of Christians support, 980
    How families support, 789
    Prospers in Church, 569
    Purge from Church, 46
    Societal blind eye towards, 698
    Sometimes good emerges, 689
    Succeeds when good doesn't act, 1000
    Succeeds when good is silent, 1001
    Turned to good, 378
    See Understanding
Evil, Exposing
    See Naming Names
Evildoers, Identifying, 546
Evolution, 218, 985
Excluded from Heaven
    List of who is cast out, 38
Excuses for Sin
    Jesus says you have none, 236
Exegesis
    Definition, 178
    Exodus (21:22-25), 745
    Graphic, 743
Exegete
    Definition, 178
Exhaust, 428
Exoteric, 19
Expectation, Fearful, 60
Expose
    Works of darkness, evil, 795
Extortioners, 39
Ezra
    Dialogue with God, salvation, 1032
    Prays for mankind, 1033
Faith
    Activate, 657
    As-If principle, 536
    Found on Christ's return? 999
    Graduated, 143
    Grows by, 583
    Grows by hearing Word, 2
    Grows when heart commits, 2
    In faith v. in law, 624
    Individual's, 502
    Mystery of, 452, 491

Copyright 2005 Edward G. Palmer, All Rights Reserved.

Book of Edward—Appendix J

Index

Faith (Continued)
    One-way, 495
    Outcome of, 639
    Rahab's, 85
    Realm of, 109
    v. Lawlessness graphic, 658
    Without works, oxymoron, 998
Faithful
    Those called, 25
    Until death, 2
    Unto death, 170
Falling Short
    v. Willful sin, 9
False Teachings, 80
False Witness
    See Rationalization
Family
    Can skew rational judgment, 238
    Cults split up, 15
    Moral duty to care for, 906
    Political solution, 916
FDA Attack, 540
Fear
    From uncertainty, 64
    Reason for, 334
    Sincere, 2
    The Gift of Fear, 771
Fear of God
    Stops sin, 320
Fear of LORD
    Beginning of wisdom, 171
Fearful
    Certain expectation, God, 62
    Expectation, 8
    Experiences, 62
    Willful sinners, should be, 8
Fearless, 496
Federalist Papers, 914
Feeding Tube, 506
Fellowship, 76
    Lost, 892
    Means practice from heart, 92
    Return to v. salvation, 8
    The Father, 7
    With God and HIS Son, 655
Fellowship, God, 83
Fences
    Let God define, 12
Fifty Percent Factor, 922, 977
    Christian vote, 1010
    National vote, 1011
    v. Many and few teaching, 1015
Fig Tree
    Unrepentant, 51
Filled, By God
    With skills & understanding, 174
Fire Insurance, 10
First Fruits
    Money pitch, 192
First Love Fellowship
    Salvation message, 388
Fleece Test, 299
Flesh, 74
    Definition, 485
    Shedding it, 505
Focus, 630
Food Laws, 515
Foolish
    Extricating God, 848
    Not doers of word, 997
Forgetting
    False doctrine, 1016
    Principle, 55
    Without confronting sin, 55
Forgiven
    All sins, myth, 8
Forgiveness
    False doctrine, 1016
    False God of, 35
    Limits to, 56
    Not an option with repentance, 55
    Requires repentance, 54
    Total, 29
Forgotten
    Righteousness, 412
    Wickedness, 412

Copyright 2005 Edward G. Palmer, All Rights Reserved.

Book of Edward—Appendix J

Index

Former
    Conduct, 30
Fornication, 821
Fornicators, 38, 836
Forsake, 656
Fraud, 617
Frederick, Paul, 552, 555, 675
Free, 135
Free Will, 12, 96, 459, 521
    God respects your, 97
Friend
    God v. world, 16, 418
    Not condemned graphic, 402
Friend, Respecting
    Discussion, 400
Friend, True, 399
Friends
    Choose carefully, 139
    Giving some up, 446
Friendship
    With God & Jesus, 413
Friendship, God's, 402
Fruits
    Expose evil people, 10
    Worthy of repentance, 10
Fruits of Spirit, 96
Gemara, 367
Get A Life, 33
Getting Close To God
    Church evolution, graphic, 560
Gideon, 6
Gift
    Insulting God, 8
    Of Christ, 8
Gift of Jesus
    Characteristics, lists of, 488
    Earthly attributes, 489
    Fellowship attributes, 488
    Greatest, 452
    Heavenly attributes, 489
    "In Christ" attributes, 489
    Salvation attributes, 488
Gift of Sex, 785

Gifts
    Carry responsibilities, 7
    Taking for granted, 8
Giving
    Not out of necessity, 670
    Principle, 672
Glorifying
    God v. self, 30
Gnostic Texts
    Discussion, 477
Go Directly To God, 679
Goads, 31
God
    Abominations to, 374
    Acknowledging exists, 249
    Activist or pacifist discussion, 175
    Alpha & Omega, 288
    Answers Ezra's prayer, 1034
    Appoints terror over, 947
    Calls His people, 24
    Comforts us, 499
    Created heaven for only a few, 1032
    Desires mercy not sacrifice, 624
    Doesn't call everyone, 97
    Doesn't change, 133
    Eternal character, 314
    Face hidden, 317
    Friend, 7
    Has plans for you, 521
    Hates, 691
    Inhabits praises of His people, 18
    Is Light, 487
    Jealous, 363
    Lament, His, 319
    Logic for punishing sinners, 323
    Loves children, 742
    Makes a way, 496
    Manifested to humans, 634
    Metaphysical nature, 341
    Nine basic attributes, 315
    No pity, 320
    Not author of confusion, 295
    Not God of the dead, 1018

Index

God (Continued)
    Of Jews, Christians & Muslims, 314
    Partiality, none to those who, 891
    Punishes, 362
    Quran dialogue, God & Christ, 1012
    Rewards, 362
    Sends good and bad, 538
    Seven Spirits, 265, 301
    Seven teachings from Christ, 1014
    Sovereignty, 381
    Standard of sin, 328
    Taken out of our lives & society, 239
    The Father, 7
    Values HIS friends, 403
    Wanting to please, 894
    Worries (no), 358
    See Trinity doctrine
God, Places
    Understanding in heart, 428
    Wisdom in mind, 428
God, Searches
    Heart, 428
God, Tests
    Heart and mind, 428
    Righteous, 428
God, Those of
    Hear HIS Words, Obey, 415
God, Wants
    Whole heart, 435
God's
    Big picture, 24
    Book of Remembrance, 665
    Enemy, 630
    Group, no judgment graphic, 1008
    Protection, 524
    Soft inner voice, 762
    Word, don't compromise it, 666
God's Balances, 89
God's Son
    True meaning of Jesus, vi
God's Spirit
    Inside you, 147
God's Ways, 109

Godliness, Riches, 589
Godly, Ungodly
    Contrasted, 166
Gods, 269
Good Man's Reward, 362
Good News, 460
Good or Bad, 686, 687
Good Works
    Alone are rejected by Christ, 107
Gospel of Christ
    Repent, for the kingdom of God is near, 1020
Gospel of Kingdom
    Preached in the entire world, 1026
Gospel of Mary, 479
Gospel of Philip, 479, 524
    Get life before you die, 504
    Jesus' death, 503
Gospel of Thomas, 478
Gospel of Truth, 479, 654, 655
Gospel, Christ's, 125
Government, Evil
    No Christian duty to, 954
Grace, 101
    Cheap, 224
    Cheap, apostasy, 133
    Election of, 228
    Perverted, 35
    Sufficient, 102
Gracious
    God's choice, 492
Graduate
    Spiritually to, 26
Graham, Billy, 310
Greater
    God greater than Jesus, 195
Greatest Gift of Jesus
    Discussion, 474
    God's Fellowship, 477
Green, Steve (song)
    Called to be HIS light, 985
    People Need The Lord, 979
Grieving, 513

Copyright 2005 Edward G. Palmer, All Rights Reserved.

Book of Edward—Appendix J

Index

Guard Your Heart, How, 754
Gunnysack, 499, 500
Habits, Bad, 516, 518
Hagee, John, 255
   Bible basis of trinity doctrine, 256
   Citations don't support trinity, 277
   Orthodox conflict of interest, 257
   Prophecy Study Bible, 255
   Salvation message, 388
   Trinity explanation, 255
Hallmark of Believer, 29
   Humility, 30
   Repentance, 30
Hamilton, Alexander, 914
Hammond, Mac, 608, 612
Hands
   Laying on, 3
Happenstance, 61
Happiness, 12
Hate
   A time for, 743
   Christians, supposed to, 691
   Defined, 693
   God's perspective, 691
   List of what to, 745
   Mind v. heart discussion, 696
   Speech, Canada, 922
Hateful, 691
   Per se v. obeying God, 694
Hatred
   Evil, fear of God instills, 692
   For God, 686
   Hate wickedness, 36
Head, 4
Healing
   12 Cancer considerations, 541
   Appointed time to die, 509
   Body is Temple, 515
   Cellular death, 539
   Cellular level, 520
   Death cheated, 534
   Death cheated temporarily, 535
   Food & cellular level, 543
   Gift of heavenly mansion, 544
   God not a slot machine, 532
   God's sovereignty over life, 526
   God's choice, 502
   Individual's faith plays role, 527
   Individual's role in, 520
   Jesus didn't heal everyone, 526
   Kathryn's heart, 532
   Lame, 533
   List of 32 issues in, 511
   Listen to body, 520
   Living will, 508
   Low stress, 497
   Man trusts in his wealth, 510
   Not always, discussion, 526
   Physically impaired choices, 508
   Role of nutrition, 539
   Those in wheel chairs, 532
   Whole armor of God, 531
Healing v. Word
   God is sovereign, 526
   Jesus asks, do you want it, 527
   Jesus didn't heal everyone, 526
Healing, Divine
   Discussion, 492
Healing, Prayer
   Formula, 536
Health
   Biblical instructions, 515
Health, Responsibility, 521
Health-Wealth God
   Perverted teaching, 92
Heart
   Bible speaks to, 20
   Broken, 499
   Call on, 110
   Changed, evidence of, 30
   Committed hearts find God, 2
   Decision & consequences, 427
   Desire, 12
   Enlarge my, 437
   Far from God, ix
   For God and task at hand, 106

Copyright 2005 Edward G. Palmer, All Rights Reserved.

Book of Edward—Appendix J

Index

Heart (Continued)
    Gatekeeper, reason, 755
    God knows, 29
    God searches, 428
    God wants yours, 319
    Guard, graphic on how to, 754
    Guard, wisdom's reason, 753
    Guarded closely, 433
    Humble, 1019
    Impenitent, 69
    Inclined towards evil, 697
    It starts with …, 2
    Laws written on, 76
    Like an on/off switch, 383
    Loyal, God searches for, 371
    Not evolutionary like faith, 2
    Of faith, 643
    Open it up, 27
    Practice from, 92
    Pure, 163, 924
    Pure, divorce scripture test, 923
    Repentance, 58
    Seat of belief, 429
    Six choices, 138
    Soul v. organ, 642
    Speaks loudly, 109
    Surrendered, controls sin, 753
    Take it to, understanding, 757
    Temple, 17
    Thought life, 155
    Thumping, 60
    Transmission analogy, 424
    v. Intellect, 680
    Whole, 2
    Willfulness, 30
    Written on by Spirit, 423
    See Faith; Thoughts
Heart For God, 402
Heart v. Mind
    Bible illustration, 682
Heart, Broken, 514
Heart, Loyal
    Understands God, 381

Heaven
    Everyone doesn't go, examples, 990
    Has selection process, 977
    Is Hitler there? 981
    Locked out of, list, 991
    No humans, myth, 980
    Violent take it by force, 989
    Who can enter, 77
    Who can't enter, 77
Hebrew
    Defined by Edward, 371
Hell
    Christians going to, ix
    Second chance theology, 980
Hell, On Earth, 439
Hermeneutics, 4
    Definition, 178
    Discussion, 179
    Principles, List, 180
Hiding, 67
Hill, Paul J., 339
    Essay on killing doctors, 342
Hilton, Paris, 802
His Presence, 498
    Perfect peace, 501
Hitler, 981
Holiness, 30
Holstein, Lana M.D.
    Magnificent Sex
        Seven Steps, 883
Holy
    Hands, 17
Holy of Holies, 7, 17
    Enter freely via Christ, viii
    With Christ, 649
    Without Christ, 649
Homophobe, 328
Homosexual, 35, 38
    Bishop, 399
    Ordained, 319
    Perverse desires, 749
    Political lobby, 227
    Practicing, 776

Index

Homosexual 10% Propaganda, 816
Homosexuality
  Abomination to God, 817
  Absolutist moral dogma, 913
  Bestiality short step away, 814
  Church endorses, 550
  Episcopal Bishops, 337
  Form of love? 223
  Gay Pride parade, Israel's, 322
  God does hate, 810
  Hollywood supports, 814
  Less than 1% of population, 852
  Marriage affects heterosexuals, 911
  Metropolitan Community Church, 810
  Mortal sin, 849
  No Constitutional right to marry, 853
  Programming children, 915
  Thirty biblical statements, 850
  Top ten cities, 851
  Truthful statistics, 850, 852
  v. Bible, 226
Honest
  True son, 230
Honesty, 20
Honor, 15
  Parents, 65
  The Son, 436
Honor, Vessel of, 808
Honoring
  Those you love, 436
Hoogenboom, James, 557
Hope, 1039
  When hopes die, 978
Horrifying, 60
Horror, 60
Hot for God, 33
Human
  Jesus Christ, 7
Humanist, 33
Humans
  None in heaven, myth, 980
Humbly
  Draw close graphic, 364

Humility, 30
  Genuine, 30
Humphrey, Hubert, 898
Hypocrites, 1017
I And Father Are One
  See Trinity Doctrine
I Can't Handle It Lord, 502
Idolaters, 38
Idolatry, 243
  Worship of Christ, 1012
  See Trinity doctrine
Illustrations, List of, 1092
Immoral
  President Clinton, Senate, 234
Impartially
  Father judges, 50
Impunity
  Support evil, myth, 980
In Christ, 486
  Those, died to willful sin, 333
In His Presence
  Fullness of Joy, viii
  Pressing In, viii
In Spirit, 423
In The Ground Doctrine, 286
Incarnate, Word v. God, 248
Incest, Lot's daughters, 749
Indoctrination, 13
Inerrant, 94
Infallibility, 94
Infallible
  No Hebrew or Greek root, 116
Infidel, 14
Influence
  God's, 574
  Misleading, God sent, 677
  Satan's, 574
Iniquity
  See Lawlessness
Injustice, 690
  Chuck Schuldt, 958
  Edward fined for telling truth, 960
  Rooted in lack of self control, 967

Copyright 2005 Edward G. Palmer, All Rights Reserved.

Book of Edward—Appendix J

Index

Inner Peace, 63
Inner Voice
   How to know it is God's, 143
Innocent Blood, 352
Inspiration, 94
Instruction Guide
   Living breathing, 29
Instructions
   Before leaving earth, 23, 975
   Christ to disciples, travel light, 15
   Don't mess with God's Word, 193
   Eight prayer, 317
   Feed my sheep [the Word], 590
   For Doctors and Pharmacists, 515
   From God about abortion, 347
   Jesus speaks on tithe, 616
   Married sex, 823
   Mercy, 740
   Nurture baby, 712
   Prayer, 312
   Prophet's, 343
   Ruling over sin, 751
   Sabbath rituals annulled, 650
   Sexual intimacy, 557
   Solomon, "get on with life," 314
   Solomon, "have two goals," 544
   Timothy on right v. wrong, 120
Insulted
   Spirit of Grace, 8
Integrity, 899
Intellect
   Insufficient, 70
Intentions
   God examines, 349
Irony, 752
Islamic Leaders, 797
Islamists, 797
   Shedding of innocent blood, 946
Israel
   Gay pride parade, 322
Itching Ears, 578
Jackie, 63
   Aunt Bernice, 505
   Book dedicated to, vi
   Bravery, 502
   Character perceptions, 607
   Christian education board, 548
   Church disagreement, 559
   Cousin's sudden death, 510
   Death, 313
   Death a blessing, 513
   Divine healing, 493
   Dog Annie, 503
   Edward painted room, 684
   Edward's first kiss, 433
   Elk River Assembly, 558
   Eulogy, 1072
   Expectations, 894
   Faith developed, 548
   Family arrives in Elk River, 548
   Father's colon cancer, 537
   Final thoughts, 1069
   Flabbergasted, 551
   Garden, 518
   Glen, first son died, 703
   Healing prayer, 313
   Heavenly wings, June 3, 2003, vi
   Her friend, 399
   Honor her memory, 384
   Knew where she was going, 420
   Last breath, 420
   Last days, 314
   Laying on hands, 529
   Love for, deep in heart, 642
   Married at seventeen, 821
   Miss me Ed? 384
   Mountain to climb, 539
   Move to Elk River, 449
   Nakedness concern, 783
   No artificial life machines, 506
   Notice of cancer, 170
   One with Edward, 316
   One with God, 316
   Opened heart to others, 727
   Paint bedroom request, 436
   Perfect peace experience, 501

Index

Jackie (Continued)
   Predestined to marry Edward, 441
   Prophecy of death, 439
   Ring around Edward's heart, 435
   Rose before she died, 504
   Second Christmas without, 978
   Sex talks with kids, 839
   Smoking, 516
   Soul departure, 420
   Soul left body, 503
   Soul-bond, 502
   Spiritual presence, 893
   Transcending earthly concerns, 501
   Tubal ligation, 856
   Uncle Earl, 505
   Vietnam War letters, 682
   Wanted a dozen children, 724
   Wedding ring symbolism, 433
   Wife of thirty-nine years, vi
Jacob
   Gave God his heart, 65
Jay, 386
Jesus Christ
   Ancestor Perez, incest, 726
   Brother, IF, 300
   Destroyed Church hierarchy, 646
   Did what God told him to do, 127
   Discussion of humanity, 484
   Divided on the cross, 505
   Doesn't change, 133
   Edward's brother, 127
   Gap in life, 24
   Gentleness, 96
   Has God's Seven Spirits, 303
   Human sacrifice on cross, 292
   Instructions from God, 247
   Know him? 279
   Lying? 129
   Made like all men, 291
   Non-characteristics, table, 461
   Not wealthy, 15
   Obedient to God, 487
   Obeys God, 252
   Only part of God's plan, 490
   Preached kingdom gospel, 1020
   Purpose was to preach kingdom, 1028
   Rejects Christians, 3
   Represented God, 127
   Salvation criteria, 130
   Sanctifies to obedience, 293
   Spoke for God, 127
   Stupid? Idiot? 206
   Talks to self as God? 283
   Teaches everyone doesn't go, 990
   Was a poor man, 661
   Words of, 136
   Worshipped? 281
Jesus' God, 196
Jew
   Real, from heart, 64
Jews
   Hiding, 78
Job
   Chose God when tested, 168
Journey, 58
Joy
   From testing, 75
   Fullness, 75
Judge
   Edward's apostleship, 127
   God judges those outside, 47
   Good v. evil, God, 362
   Righteously, 357
   Those inside church, 46, 359
   With God's righteousness, 357
Judge, Don't
   Those outside Church, 359
Judged
   According to our ways, 338
   Individuals v. church, 95
   Not. Already passed to life, 1002
   On your last day, 1002
Judging
   Discussion, 339, 352
   Episcopalians, 338
   First two steps, 355

Index

Judgment
   Colored, human terms, 65
   Do no injustice, 960
   God gave to Christ, 1004
   Impending, fearful, 63
   Individuals weighed on balance, 1009
   Making v. passing, 598
   Not by ceremonial laws, 628
   Rational, 220
Judgment, Rational
   Part of wisdom, 220
Judgmental
   v. Judging, 356
Judgmentalism, 380
   Discussion, 385
Justice, 897
   Court rules deny, 685
   Legal system graphic, 957
   Not in immoral societies, 957
   Not with a public defender, 958
Karen, vii, 599
Kaseman, Jim, 608, 609, 612
Kazantzakis, Nikos
   Last Temptation of Christ, 206
Kennedy, John, 234
Kerry, John F, 701, 901
   Lies, 955
Killing Abortion Doctors
   Paul J. Hill's rationalization, 341
King James Bible
   15th translation, 111
   Errant, 98
   Errors discussed, 113
   Says God repents, error, 114
King, Martin Luther, 1001
Kingdom
   Angels sort out wicked, 1023
   Be counted worthy of, 1031
   Belongs to God, not Jesus, 1019
   Belongs to humble hearts, 1019
   Belongs to righteous, 1019
   Better without limb than hell, 1027
   Created only for a few, 1032
   Dragnet gathers good and bad, 1023
   Everyone in is greater than John, 1021
   Father's, 7
   Flesh and blood cannot inherit, 1030
   Forgiving those who repent, 1024
   God answers Ezra's prayer, 1034
   God preserves righteous for, 1031
   God's pleasure to give us, 1028
   Has Eunuchs, 1025
   Has righteousness standard, 1019
   Jesus commanded we preach it, 1020
   Jesus culls out unrighteous, 1027
   Jesus explains fields, seeds, etc, 1022
   Jesus gathers & delivers to God, 1030
   Jesus says it is at hand, 1027
   Jesus' Gospel, 1020
   Jesus' purpose was to preach, 1028
   Keys, 989
   Keys, Jesus is Son of God, 1024
   Keys, who knows Jesus is Son, 1024
   Life, focus, 1018
   Like a mustard seed, 1022
   Like a wedding, 1026
   Like group of little children, 1025
   Like hidden treasure, 1023
   Like leaven, 1022
   Like merchant seeking pearls, 1023
   Like scribes with treasure, 1023
   Manifested from within people, 1029
   Many called, but few chosen, 1025
   Mysteries, 1021
   No visual indications, 1028
   Not eating or drinking, 1030
   Not everyone enters, 1020
   Not in words, but action, 1030
   One-way street, 1028
   Only if you do Father's will, 989
   Path has tribulations, 1029
   People pressing in, 1028
   Preach it, let dead care for dead, 1028
   Preached in the entire world, 1026
   Purged when Christ returns, 1024
   Receives all who repent, 1026

Copyright 2005 Edward G. Palmer, All Rights Reserved.

Index

Kingdom (Continued)
    Rejects 50% of some groups, 1026
    Rejects unrighteous, list, 1030
    Requires faith of child, 1024
    Requires nation bears fruit, 1026
    Requires profitable servants, 1027
    Requires repentance, 1019
    Requires surrender of control, 1025
    Requires you to be born of spirit, 1029
    Rewards the obedient, 1029
    Righteous in all nations enter, 1020
    Righteousness, peace and joy, 1030
    Satan snatches loose seeds, 1021
    Satan sows doubt & confusion, 1022
    Seek it and HIS righteousness, 1019
    Serve with reverence & fear for, 1031
    Shut out by some churches, 1026
    Signs of end times, 1029
    Unified, 1021
    Unrighteous Christians not in, 1020
    Violent take it by force, 1021
    Walk worthy of God on earth, 1030
    We eat and drink in, 1027
Kingdom of God
    Inside you, 76
Knowing, 63
Knowledge
    Beginning of, 897
    First hand, 571
    God gave Bezaleel, 171
    Head v. heart, 2
    Nutraceuticals, 540
    Second hand, opinion based, 571
Kocina, Lonny
    Media Hypnosis
        Unleashing, 572
Koran
    See Quran
Lack
    Apostles, 492
    Instruction, 492
    Knowledge, 492
    Nothing, 496

    Peace, 498
    Troubles, 499
    Understanding, 492
Laetrile and Cancer, 542
Lakewood Church
    Salvation message, 389
Lascivious
    Examples, 889
Lasciviousness, 135
    Strong'S Concordance, 806
Last Day (The), 1001
Last Temptation of Christ, 206
Law
    430 Years after covenant, 639
    Book of Law, 625
    Cannot summarily dismiss, 660
    Catchall, do what's right, 641
    Ceremonial laws, list, 628
    Commands to obey, 635
    Contract, God & Israel, 640
    Conundrum of, 624
    Discussion, 621
    Doesn't void covenant, 635
    Five distinctions in Deut., 627
    Four distinctions by David, 627
    Human issues still exist, 641
    Not for righteous, 642
    Some parts annulled, 631
    Some parts kept, commands, 631
    Some parts still active, 644
    Still matters, 591
    To those in Christ, graphic, 659
    Unto themselves, 76
Lawless
    Rejected, 567
Lawless Christians
    Rejected by Christ, 108
Lawlessness
    Practice of, 332
    Practiced, 632
    Practitioners, 4
    To those in Christ, graphic, 659
    v. Faith graphic, 658; *See* Sin

Index

Laws, Ceremonial, 640
Laws, Church, 646
Laws, Civil, 640
Laws, Marriage, 640
Laws, Sabbath, 646
   Christ annulled rituals, 649
Laws, Sexual, 645
Laws, Social, 640
Lawsuits, 568
Laying on Hands, 529
Legal System, U.S.
   Does not seek justice, 958
Length of Days, 756
Lens, False, 487
Lesbian, 35
Lesbianism
   Abomination to God, 817
   Elizabeth Stroud, 986
   Mortal sin, 849
   See Homosexuality
Let Go Let God, 9
Letter In Night
   Salvation message, 390
Lewd
   Examples, 889
   Public exposure, 832
   Strong'S Concordance, 806
Lewis, C.S.
   Mere Christianity, 481
   Original meaning of "Christian," 483
Liar, 78, 956
Licentious, 134
   Examples, 889
Licentiousness
   Ungodly turn God's Grace into, 809
Lie
   Paul says he doesn't, 73
Lies
   Pastor about money? 618
   Political programming, 955
   Under oath, 593

Life
   Belongs to God, 731
   Changed, Edward's, 548
   Die to sin, live for righteousness, 358
   Exists in womb, 715
   God's sovereignty over, 381
   Graphic, generally evil, 330
   Graphic, generally good, 329
   Graphic, God's view of sin, 331
   Graphic, on balance good, 330
   Graphic, Spirit of Christ effect, 333
   In human blood, 713
   In Word, 590
   Kingdom focused, 1018
   Live to 120, 439
   Living testament, 109
   Longevity & Genesis 6:3, 439
   Metaphysical manifestations, 451
   Proudest moment, 417
   Requires an accounting, 335
   Spiritual forces, 433
   Stack of deeds graphic, 327
   Turn from sin and live, 338
Lifespan
   Exercise, 173
Light
   Walk in, 496
Light of Life, 480
Light, God, 487
Like Mindedness, 925
Like Precious Faith
   Those called, 25
Lincoln, Abraham, 760
Live
   On every word of God, 591
Living Faith Center, 552, 553
   Deeper worship, 554
Living Word Ministries, 608
Lost Books
   List of five, 264
Lost Gospels of Christ, 477

Copyright 2005 Edward G. Palmer, All Rights Reserved.

Book of Edward—Appendix J

Index

Love
   Always a choice, 866
   Attributes of, 678
   Chronological, 643
   Covers sin, 229
   God's perspective, 691
   Godly, when dying, 507
   Long-suffering? 508
   Nine characteristics, 683
   Priority in heart, 643
   Unlimited, 643
Love Doctrine
   False, 224
Lovers of Lies, 38
Lovers of Truth
   Those who do not, ix
Lukewarm, 384
   Spewed out, 34
Lust, Unbridled, 806
Lutheran, 6
Lutzer, Erwin W.
   Seven Reasons To Trust Bible, 23
Luxuries
   Errant wealth teachings, 16
Lying, 897
   25 times a day, 83
   Clinton, 84
   Rahab, 84
Mac (Televangelist), 383
Magnificent
   Gift, 7
Maher, Bill, 778
Mail
   Is Bible your mail? 680
   Is God writing to you, 25
Manuscript, Greek, 367
Manuscript, Hebrew, 367
Marriage, 557, 846
   Bed sanctified, 796
   Divorce, God hates, 923
   Foundational Bible verse, 884
   Gay, or civil unions, 778
   Long lasting, 875
   Modern pressures, 882
   Repudiation of Gay, 916
   Same sex blessings, 370
   Sexless, 881
Marriage, Law of, 640
Martin, Ernest L.
   The Tithing Dilemma, 661
Marvel, 23
Mary
   Accepted God's Will, 70
Masoretic Text, 367
Matters
   Commandments, 634
   Commands, 634
   Obedience, 634
Matthews, Mary Beth, 546
Matthews, William Neal, 545, 546
   AFCM ruse, used, 608
   Apostate tithe teaching, 567
   Candidates for Pastor, 559
   Chuck Schuldt's accuser, 959
   Committed to fraud, 605
   Confronted by Edward, 568
   Deception, 606
   Disaffiliates AFCM, ruse, 611
   Disenfranchised congregation, 609
   Dumps AFCM after settling AG, 613
   Duped congregation, 607
   Exposed con, 602
   False Article's filings, 606
   False teacher, 564
   God's spiritual test, 559
   How he stole Solid Rock, 961
   Jeremiah 23 deception, 599
   Lacks godly reason, wisdom, 568
   New Testament Church pitch, 610
   Not impartial to congregation, 960
   Scattered flock of God, 600
   Shut down God's ministries, 566, 995
   State filings don't lie, 592
   Stole God's property, 547
   Swindler, isolated events, 601
   Swindler, linear events, 601

Index

Matthews, William Neal (Continued)
    Theft, context of, 603
    Ultimate tithe perversion, 666
    Unrepentant servant of Satan, 606
    Which offering will God bless? 589
Mediator
    Christ, 22
    None but Christ, 651
    Only one, 22
Mediocre, Christians, 440
Mercy, 740
    God's choice, 492
    Limit to God's, 90
Message
    Apostate pulpit, UCC, 549
    Edward's, 368
    God's to Belshazzar, 90
    I never knew you, 3
    Many Christians will go to hell, ix
    Tithe, of Satan, 677
Message of Jesus
    Repent, 29
Message of John
    Repent, 29
Message of Prophets
    Repent, 29
Message, Christ's, 124
Message, Salvation
    Christ did not change it, 125
Metaphysical, 12
Middle East Conflict, 379
Miles, Jack, 210
    Christ, A Crisis in the Life of God
    Trinity rationalization, 289
Mind
    Laws written on, 76
Mind v. Heart
    Bible illustration, 682
    Graphic, 695
Mind, Attributes of, 428
Mind, Sound, 172
Mind, Strong
    Given by God, 172

Mind-Body Separation, 497
Ministers, Unfit, 677
Minnesota Council of Churches, 549
Miracles, 502
    Zone, 166
Miscarriage, 678
Mishnah, 367
Missionary, 65
Mistaken, 173
Mistakes, 142
Misunderstanding
    Caused by man-made doctrine, 182
Molestation, Priest's, 592
Money, 492
Moral Values, 898
    Abortionite opinion, 898
    Christians, 50% upside down, 990
    Commingling, 948
    Exercise, 905
    God's perspective, tables, 919
    Nation divided, graph & stats, 908
Morality
    Biblical strategy, 912
    Christians don't agree, why, 910
    Decline started with prayer ban, 927
    National foundation in families, 951
    Political will, 940
Morality of Rights, 913
Morningstar Ministry
    Salvation message, 389
Mortal Sin, 838
Moses
    Burning bush, 66
Motives, 336
Mouth
    Immoral woman's, 749
Mouthing Jesus
    Not a sign of those saved, 4
Muhammad, 370
Murderers, 38
Muscles, Spiritual, 105
Muslim
    Defined by Edward, 371

Index

Mysterious Plan, 452
Myth
   Everybody needs Jesus, 1039
Mythology
   Christ's exclusive salvation, 158
   Routinely taught at pulpits, x
Myths
   Rationalization, 227
   Turning away from truth, 227
Nakedness
   Familial relationships, 780
   Rules summarized, 784
Name It, Claim It, 532
Naming Names, 546
   Bible examples, 596
   Exposing evil, 591
   Public rebuke, 592
Narrow Path, Imperfect
   Defined, graphic, 154
Narrow Path, Life
   Defined, graphic, 153
Nathanson, Bernard
   Eclipse of Reason, 705
Nazi, 78
Nebuchadnezzar
   Dream, 176
New Beginning, 495
New Covenant, 250
   Holds individuals responsible, 322
New King James
   Default translation used, iii
   Satanic, not, 254
New Life, 58, 313
   Choice, 132
New Man, 71
Newborn, 3
News
   Staged, 572
Nicolaitans
   Perverted Paul's teachings, 134
Nightingale, Earl
   Strangest Secret, 449, 766
No Excuse, 311, 461
   For willful sin, 468
Non-Christians
   Going to Heaven, 2
Nonsense, 172
Norman, 498, 499, 500, 537
NOVA
   Miracle of Life, 711
Nowthen Alliance, 551, 675
   Return to, 555
Nutraceuticals, 541
Nutrition
   Discussion, 539
O'Donnell, Rosie, 849
Obedience, 245
   Demonstrates you understand, 203
   Jesus sanctifies us to, 293
   Lifestyle, 30
Obedient, 50
   Help from God and Christ, 109
   Jesus Christ, 487
Obedient, to God
   Elizabeth and Zacharias, 187
Obey
   Command to, 27
   God v. Man, 360
Offensive, 10
Old Man, 71
Old Testament
   Dismissed, 101
Omega, 287
One
   God, Christ and you, 146
One God, 81, 243
Oneness
   Spiritual, 81
One-Way, 495
Opinion
   God or Edward's, 50
Opinions, 368
Opposite
   Devotion v. sin, 29
   Good v. evil, 29

Index

Oral Sex, 813
   Clinton, 773
Ordained
   Book of Edward, 2
Ordinances, Kept
   Elizabeth and Zacharias, 187
Orwell's 1984, 600
Overcoming, Earthly Life
   Believe that Christ is Son, 128
Ownership, 82
Oxymoron, 546
   Democrat Christians? 975
Parable
   Lost Coin, 53
   Lost Sheep, 52
   Lost Son, 53
   Rich Young Ruler, 79
Paracelsus, 198, 222
Paradise, 283, 503
Paradise, Statement
   Opposes trinity, 284
Parents
   Dishonoring, 580
Parse, 128
Parsley, Rod
   Apostate teachings, 190
   False teaching discussion, 191
Passed Into Life, Already, 1003
Passing Through, 34
Pastor
   Sin against God, 68
Path of Life, 75
Path, Light On
   Discussion, 416
Patience
   From testing, 75
Patient
   God is, 34
Patty, vii, 60
   Dylan, 714
   Dylan's wings, 537
   Fourth grade, 799
   Luke's fall, 61
   Marriage, 834
   Shoebox, 717
   Truck dent, 496
Paul's Teachings
   Not higher than Christ's, 181
   Not higher than God's, 181
Paula, vii, 510, 893, 894
   Public confession of faith, 553
PC Talk
   See ; Kerry, John F
Peace, 496, 501
   Graphic, 497
   Perfect, 75
   Psalm 34, 498
Pelosi, Nancy, 986
Penner, Clifford & Joyce
   The Gift of Sex, 785
People, Good, 1004
Perfect, 87
   Conditions, 313
   Conditions, discussion, 314
   Jesus asks, want to be, 79
   Law of LORD, 627
   Not on our own accord, 101
   Only in Christ, 101
   Peace, 496
   Sacrifice, 315
   Sell everything, follow me, 82
   To God "In Christ," 777
Perfect Day
   Light of Sabbath inside, 654
Perfection
   False doctrine, 99
   Not God's expectation, 83
Perfection Doctrine
   False, 103
Perish, People
   Not lovers of truth, 225
Permissible, 657
Persecution, 5
Pharmaceutical Attack, 540
Philosophy, 22

Index

Phinehas
   Rationalized to kill doctors, 345
Picture, God's, 361
   David saw, 376
   Ezekiel saw, 377
   Graphic, 380
   Joseph saw, 378
   More than you see, 379
   Paul saw, 378
Picture, Whole, 360
Piety, 906
Piper, Modern, 800
Pleasing
   Those you love, 436
Pleasure, 764
Pleasures
   From God, 75
Politicians
   Elitists, not enlightened, 941
   Public persona, fails at judgment, 940
Politics
   A debased Supreme Court, 929
   Able bodied people, 905
   Appoints terror over nations, 947
   Art of lying, 954
   Biblical message for U.S., 968
   Biblical morality, 912
   Black monolithic vote, 902
   Christian voting data, 909
   Christian's big picture, 898
   Christians should be like minded, 926
   Christians, no duty to obey evil
     government, leaders or laws, 954
   Church attendance factor, 908
   Confused Christians, 910
   Constitution for godly people, 952
   Control of House, table, 932
   Control of Presidency, table, 934
   Control of Senate, table, 933
   Corporations are tax collectors, 904
   Decades of Democrat policies, 916
   Democracies commit suicide, 951
   Democrat Christians? 975
   Democrat intentions, 917
   Democrat policies altered mores, 940
   Democrat Senators' immorality, 955
   Democrat societal changes, 969
   Democrats allowed abortion law, 939
   Democrats allowed prayer ban, 937
   Democrats responsible for moral
     decay in United States, 931
   Democrats' legacy is immoral, 970
   Disappointed Democrats, 901
   Duplicitous, 941
   Edward's seed of injustice test, 922
   Enlightenment, 941
   Events in 1960, 935
   Events in 1961, 936
   Events in 1962, 937
   Events in 1972, 938
   Events in 1973, 939
   Federalist Papers, 914
   Feeding at public trough, 899
   First Amendment, 945
   Founder's advice, 970
   George Washington and God, 942
   God hates divorce, 923
   God sends terror, 946
   God's moral values, tables, 919
   God's v. man's priorities, 976
   Humphrey's moral test, 922
   Immoral policies, 911
   Immoral to create dependency, 915
   Impact of Gay marriage, 911
   Impeachment of judges, 927
   Jewish monolithic vote, 907
   Judicial activism, 930
   Kennedy's "rights of man" era, 928
   Kerry's repeated lies, 955
   King David's advice, 973
   Legislature impeachment reality, 972
   Lessons from Washington, God, 944
   Liars go to hell, 956
   Liberty, John Adams, 950
   Likened to ten virgins, vote, 980
   Moral decline after prayer ban, 938

Index

Politics (Continued)
   Moral duty to care for family, 906
   Moral governance uncertain, 970
   Moral v. immoral parties, 904
   Morality of rights, example, 913
   Morality v. moral "rights," 912
   Morals, "melting pot," 930
   Multiculturalism v. moral unity, 948
   Nation morally divided, data, 908
   No justice in immoral society, 957
   Pelosi on Marriage amendment, 986
   Philosophical difference, 903
   Policies without spiritual weight, 995
   Problems in soak rich strategy, 903
   Rathergate, 956
   Real results for real Christians, 974
   Red state voters, 901
   Rugged individualism, 905
   Separation of church issue, 918
   Smarter to elect two lawyers? 901
   Spiritually united nation, 950
   Stupid to reelect Bush? 901
   Supreme Court ban on prayer, 927
   U.S. 50% towards anarchy, 953
   U.S. founded by Christians, 914
   U.S. History, people of faith, 945
   U.S. made a covenant with God, 943
   U.S. moral foundation, lost, 944
   Virtue, public, 951
   What both major parties support, 903
   What Democrats support, 902
   Yoked with unbelievers, 949
   See End Times
Poor, 897
Pornography, 793
   Blue Chip's profiting, 803
   China and Google, 806
   Distribution, 804
   Meg Ryan, 794
   Soft v. Hard, 795
   Used to be isolated, 802
Possible
   To live (ruled) by Spirit, 73

Possible, All Things, 449
Power
   Released to committed hearts, 12
Power Play
   Pastor's, 21
Practical Christianity, 20
Practice, 9
   Checklist, 88
   Out of, 76
   Righteous like Christ, 325
Practices
   Righteousness is righteous, 45
Practitioner of Lies, 38
Praise
   From God, not men, 64
Pray
   Always, 538
   For God's Will in matter, 538
   Jesus says -- "to Father," 280
   See Trinity Doctrine
Pray, Without Ceasing, 120
Prayer
   A Real Salvation Prayer, 1043
   Don't lose hope, 538
   For non-deadly sin, 517
   Healing, 494
   Instructions from Christ, 317
   Intimate, with God, 177
   Jesus prayed to God, 205
   Model, 312
   Nature of, changes, 537
   Perpetuity, 529
   Private, 316
   The New School Prayer, 987
   To Father, 316
   Vain repetitions, 316
Prayer of Faith, 531
   Defined, 536
Prayer of Jabez, 57
Prayer, Healing
   Hands, laying on, 529
   Hezekiah's, 511
   How to, 517

Index

Prayer, Healing (Continued)
   List of verses, 519
   Thy will v. demand, 512
Prayers
   Answered, 176
Preach
   The Word, 97, 582
Precepts, God's
   Gives understanding, 171
Precious, 7
Predestined
   For good or evil, 374
Pregnancy Myth, 704
Presence
   Of God, 17
Present Moment, 499
Preserved
   Those called, 26
Pressing In, 17
   Draw close graphic, 364
   In His Presence graphic, 365
Priorities
   Godly, 13
Priority
   Church usurps God's, 13
   Word first over church or pastor, 1042
Problems, 499
Process
   Romans (10:8-10), 5
   Salvation - 2 Steps, 5
Promise
   First Bible, honor parents, 65
Prophecy
   Fulfilled, ix
   Living in Bible times, like, 925
   United States, 925
Prophecy, Mythology
   Fulfilled, x
   Mythology will be embraced, x
Prophecy, Truth
   Fulfilled, x
   Truth will be ignored, x
Prophesy, To, 107

Prophet
   True, test, 342
Prophets, False, 321
Propitiation, 100, 485
Protection, God's, 524-525
Protest
   Christians, Christ's rejection, 3
Providence, 61
Providential, 313
Pulpits
   Jesus speaks, 562
Punishment
   For sin, certain, 320
   God's logic explained, 323
Pure, 45
Purgatory
   List of verses, mythology, 278
Purge Evil
   From amongst you, 48
Purifies, 45
Qualifications, Ministry, 111
Question
   Most fundamental of all, 978
Quran, 370
   God dialogues with Christ, 1012
   Jesus supports worship teaching, 1013
Rahab, 85
   God viewed her lies differently, 87
Rape, 728
Rapture, 999
Rapturous Delight, 881
Rathergate, 956
Rational
   Definition, 223
   Not without knowledge of God, 221
Rationalization
   Clinton's Oral sex, 236
   Close relationships cause, 238
   Debt, use of, 240
   Discussion starts, 204
   Edward's, 225
   God of forgiveness only, 224
   Graphic, 222

Copyright 2005 Edward G. Palmer, All Rights Reserved.

Book of Edward—Appendix J

Index

Rationalization (Continued)
    Inversely proportional to truth, 222
    Is false witness, 241
    Old theological dig, graphic, 215
    Opposite of truth, 217
Rationalize
    Definition, 223
    Not with God, 237
Reason, 753
    Dialogue with God, 568
    Discussion, 219
    Five facts about God's law, 755
    God expects v. rationalization, 236
    God speaks, 454
    Keeps emotions in check, 755
    Keeps priorities straight, 238
    Mind controls, 756
    Sign of godly character, 98
    Tested by close relationships, 238
Reasoned
    Ability to be, 21
Rebuke, Public, 592
Reeves, Christopher, 508
Refocus, 498
Rejected
    Astonishing, 4
    Christian leaders, 4
    Those who cast out demons, 3
    Those who did mighty wonders, 3
    Those who prophesied, 3
Rejoice, 513
Religion & Ethics News, 909
Remembrance
    Let it rest too, 514
Remission, Sins, 468
Repent, 94
    Definition, 37
    Message of Jesus Christ, 460
    Message of John the Baptist, 460
    Message of Prophets, 460
    Unchanging Message of God, 460
Repentance, 460
    Daily prayer, 57
    From the heart, 58
    Graphic, 157
    Sincere, 29
    Specific prayer, 57
    True, 30
Reprove, 788
    Failure to, 694
    Sin of children, 834
Republican Party
    Moral governance uncertain, 970
Respect, 363
Respect For God
    Discussion, 437
Respirator, Artificial, 505
Responsible, 7
Resurrection, 492
    Before death, 504
    Body, 422
    Body, comes later, 504
    Not of the dead, 1018
    Of righteous, 35
    Spirit, 422
Revelation, Divine, 368
Revilers, 38
Rhetoric, 96
Riches
    Danger in, 82
Righteous
    Abraham, 187
    Close to God, 107
    Elizabeth, 187
    Job, 187
    Like Christ, 567
    Only IF you obey God, 346
    Satan's ministers appear, 585
    Scribe, 493
    Those who hate, condemned, 897
    Zacharias, 187
Righteous People
    Afflictions, 499
    Are like Christ, 495
    Belong to God, vii, 9, 54
    God shows no favoritism, vii

Copyright 2005 Edward G. Palmer, All Rights Reserved.

Book of Edward—Appendix J

Index

Righteous People (Continued)
    Jesus did not come for, vii
    Uncommitted to Christ, vii
    Without Christ, 54
Righteous Way
    A one-way street, 324
Righteousness
    Agents of, 228
    Awake to, 395
    Branch, 600
    Counsel, stand up for truth, 959
    Distorted Christian message, vi
    Doing what's right, graphic, 638
    God's expectation, 324
    God's v. man's, 354
    Graphic, minimum standard, 106
    His, 57
    How to make the minimum, 790
    Kingdom requirement, vii
    Live for, 358
    Minimum, 4
    Minimum standard, 164, 789
    Need to practice, 9
    Satan's ministers disguised in, 149
    Scribes & Pharisees lacked min, 107
    True, 30
    What about, 3
    See Practice
Righteousness, Self, 376
Rightly Divide Word, 99
Rituals, 626
Robinson, V. Gene, 370
    Anglican Church, beyond repair, 857
    Condemned by Word, 792
    Great apostasy, 455
Roe v. Wade, 354
    Abortion stigma removed, 698
    Unintended consequences, 688
Rule over Sin, 750
Rules
    Spirit helps us live up to them, 337
Rules of Life, 326
Ryan, Meg, 794, 795

Nude images, 798
Sabbath
    Dwells inside believers, 654
    Free from physical aspects, 654
    Jesus broke laws, 652
    Jesus Lord of, 652
    Jesus taught new things, 653
    Saturday, 651
    Voices of prophets read, 653
Sabbath Commandment, 649
    You can't comply with it, 651
Sabbath Instructions, 650
Sacrifice
    Human or hoax, 292
Sadness, Unimaginable, 499
Saints
    Called to be, 25
Salient
    True repentance, 44
Salvation, 372
    Apart from Christ, 387
    Belongs to God, 157
    Condemned by own choices, 1036
    Did not arrive with Jesus, 190
    Discussion of mythology, 158
    Doesn't rest in Christ alone, 1004
    Exists prior to Jesus, 247
    Ezra prays for mankind, 1033
    Five half-baked teachings, 388
    God explains "few" to Ezra, 1032
    God gave to the Lamb, 157
    Jesus rejects lawless, 996
    Jesus rejects uncaring, 995
    Light of Sabbath inside, 654
    New walk for rest of life, 495
    Paul's formula, 5
    Paul's recipe, 397
    Responsibilities, 792
    Righteousness required, 107
    Saved by own choices, 1036
    The wise and foolish, 997
    See Process
Salvation Prayer, 1043

Index

Salvation v. Word
    148 NKJV verses, 415
    Calling on LORD v. Lord, 394
    Christ only part of God's plan, 490
    Everyone righteous lives, 413
    Ezekiel Chapter Eighteen, 410
    Five teachings of Jesus, 406
    Graphic "it's about God," 407
    Jesus explains belief in him, 408
    Only in Christ is apostasy, 407
    Requires obedience, 394
    Six teachings of Jesus, 409
    Twenty-five biblical teachings, 414
Salvation, False
    Discussion, 382
    For world v. willful sinners, 405
    John 3:16 "Christ is God," 405
    John 14:6-7 "through me," 405
    Limits to calling on Jesus, 394
    Line forms to right graphic, 404
    Primary cause, 398
    Second major aspect, 404
Sanctified
    Those called, 25
    To obedience by Christ, 293
Sanctify
    Definition, 192
Sandbagger
    See Gunnysack
Satan
    Angel of light, 545
    Doesn't care about, 498
    Doesn't care about unrighteous, 102
    Foothold, 548
    Has a church for you, 577
    Influence, 573
    Switching sides strategy, 800
Saved
    By one's own choices, 1036
    Everyone is not, 97
Scalia, Antonin, 930
Schiavo, Terry, 506, 507, 509
Schism, 399
School
    Politically incorrect prayer, 987
Schuldt, Chuck, 958
Scorsese, Martin, 206
Scribe
    Edward, 493
Scripture
    Carefully observe it, 152
    Doesn't support trinity, 278
    Don't add to it, 152
    Don't take away from it, 152
    God opened their minds, 203
    Hierarchy, false, 181
    Opened understanding, 415
    Opinion connects dots, illus, 118
    Scripture connects dots, illus, 117
    Speak for itself, 117
    Teaches against trinity, table, 305
    Where does it rank, 455
Search
    Find God, 177
Second Coming
    Faith found by Christ? 999
Secret
    Evil acts, 547
    Kingdom of God, 452
    Lawlessness, 452
    Plan, 452
    See Apocryphon
Seek
    God's kingdom & righteousness, 1019
Self-Centered, 996
Self-Talk, 384
Senate, U.S.
    Rationalized lawlessness, 234
Separation
    Soul-spirit from body, 505
Servants
    Those called, 26
Serve
    Choose whom you, 138
    Christ says God only, 126
    God alone, 1013

Index

Seven Spirits of God, 301
   Given to Jesus, 303
   List, 304
Sex
   16-year old males, auto pilot, 839
   58-year old males, auto what, 840
   A private matter, 900
   Abortion as birth control, 856
   Alcohol, tobacco, 883
   Always a choice, 866
   Anal sex, 813
   Archaic Bible terms, 767
   Asexual people, 815
   Automatic body responses, 877
   Bestiality, 814
   Birth control, 856
   Bodily discharges, 826
   Body pressures, internal, 822
   Canadian TV therapist, 824
   Choice, vessel of honor, 808
   Church teachings, 764
   Cohabitation, 833
   Control, what do you tell God? 890
   Dual genitalia, confusion, 815
   During menstrual cycle, 782
   During pregnancy, 826
   Ecstasy, 880
   Ejaculation v. cancer, 822
   Enraptured by wife's love, 821
   Erectile dysfunction, 841
   Evil or good, graphic, 885
   Extricating God, foolish, 848
   Facts about love, marriage, sex, 875
   Female egg supply, 825
   Foreplay, 829
   Fornication, adultery, 836
   Fornication, sex outside marriage, 821
   Freedom of married, 876
   Gateway heart choice, graphic, 866
   Getting someone drunk, 791
   God created a male and female, 808
   God's human creation, 780
   God's safe sex solution, 831
   Guilt teachings, church, 829
   How often, 881
   Human body design, pleasure, 764
   Immoral sex gate, 867
   Intimacy problems, 883
   Inviting God into bedroom, 828
   Involuntary body responses, 879
   Know your body, 785
   Loose female sexuality, 840
   Lust v. random thoughts, 765
   Magnificent sex, how to have, 883
   Male conquering mentality, 835
   Male psyche v. easy women, 833
   Male sperm, 819
   Male thinks differently after, 840
   Marriage bed sanctified, 796
   Marriage, one man, one woman, 846
   Married instructions, 823
   Masturbation, 820
   Menopause, 825
   Merriam Webster, 807
   Moral, 823
   Moral sex gate, 867
   Moral v. Immoral, 750
   Nakedness of kin, 780
   Never too old for, 821
   Nocturnal emissions, 843
   Normal male thoughts, 765
   Oral sex, 813, 828
   Parasympathetic nervous system, 878
   Passion v. compassion, 885
   Penis, autonomic response, 773
   Playboy magazine, 801
   Put excitement in, 882
   Rear entry vaginal, 825
   Reason bridle's impulses, 895
   Ruling over sin, test, 750
   Satisfied by wife's breasts, 821
   Saving virginity till marriage, 842
   Sexual pleasure, part of design, 818
   Sin control, 823
   Solitary acts, 764
   Source of church teachings, 818

Copyright 2005 Edward G. Palmer, All Rights Reserved.

Index

Sex (Continued)
    Summary of nakedness rules, 784
    Summary table, practices, 887
    Sympathetic nervous system, 878
    v. Committed hearts, 837
    Visual stimulation, 785
    Warning, 896
    When a partner has pain, 900
    Women designed to enjoy, 830
    Zone discussion, God v. Satan, 886
Sex Change, Male, 815
Sexless, 881
Sexual
    Disease, 835
    Fantasies, 785
    Self control, 774
    Unexpected encounters, 840
Sexual Immorality
    Abortionite history, 860
    Adult means porn, 788
    Big picture graphic, 842
    Biggest consequence, 864
    Cable and Satellite, 788
    Checked by reason, 755
    Clinton, Bill, 761
    Has consequences, 854
    Insults God's Grace, 796
    Internet and Google, 801
    Lasciviousness in Bible, 770
    Level I - Lewdness, 766
    Level II - Lasciviousness, 766
    Level III - Licentiousness, 766
    Lewdness in Bible, 769
    Lewdness test, 768
    Licentious in Bible, 770
    Movies, 786
    Precursors to, 773
    Stop by engaging brain, 895
    Summary of moral sex, 887
    Thought-action process, 762
    Three levels of, graphic, 766
    Traced to orthodox teachings, 774
    Training videos, 794
    Unpredictable toll, 779
    v. Perfection, 777
    Why isn't Internet coded, 802
Sexually
    Confused, gender, 812
Sexually Immoral, 38
    Die in lake of fire, 749
    Don't keep company with, 749
    Don't meet min righteousness, 793
    Outside of heaven, 749
Shameful, 567
Sharon's Sing-A-Long, 456
Shattered Nerves, 60
Shortcomings, 109
Signs
    Follow believers, 12
Silent, 10
Simpleminded
    Idea of non-discriminating, 987
Simplicity
    Genuine faith, vi
Sin
    Apostle John clarifies, 104
    Apostle John speaks, 45
    Apostle Paul clarifies, 104
    Bearing guilt by not reproving, 694
    Causing others to, 334
    Causing others, people trusted, 799
    Child not liable for parent's, 413
    Control, what do you tell God, 890
    Corporation can't justify, 798
    Covering, 591
    Deadly, 516
    Debate, all forgiven, 41
    Fear of God, 320
    God says "rule over it," 749
    God's catch all phrase, 120
    Graphic illustration, 108
    Graphic, eliminating sin, 43
    Instructions, ruling over sin, 751
    Is lawlessness, 45
    Jesus says "sin no more," 43
    Jesus speaks, 39

Index

Sin (Continued)
  Keep short list with God, 56
  Lingering, 39
  List of leading to death, 518
  Mortal, 838
  No Excuse, 311
  Not to be tolerated, 46
  Parent not liable for child's, 413
  Paul says "do not sin," 395
  Punishment, 320
  Routine control over, 752
  Standard, 328
  Standard shifts with knowledge, 121
  Still matters to God, 41
  Unintended, 100
  Unintentional, 44
  Unknown, 44, 100
  Unwillful, 100
  Willful, 100
  Woe to those who cause, 788
Sin, Definition
  Apostle James defines, 120
Sincere
  Repentance from Heart, 58
Sinking Feeling, 60
Sinner, Repentant
  Joy in heaven, 52
Sinners
  Children of devil, 45
  No place among godly, 445
  Separate yourselves from, 47
Sins
  Confess them, 356
  Die to, 358
  Keep short list, 357
Sirach, 34
Slave, 775
Slaves, 398
Slot Machine, God
  See Matthews, William
Smoking, 515
Sodomites, 38

Software, Bible
  Allows easy search for truth, 216
Solid Rock Church
  86 of 100 witnesses turned backs, 593
  Apostate doctrines, 996
  Apostate teachings, 567
  Articles manipulated, 328
  Assembly of God foreclosure, 612
  Assembly of God lawsuit, 607
  Behind the scenes, 605
  Chuck Schuldt, 958
  Den of thieves, ix, 546
  Edward seeks justice, denied, 685
  False witness, ix
  Final outcome in God's hands, 690
  Gwen, 959
  Inviting praise-worship service, ix
  Isolated events graphic, 601
  Issued stock, 605
  Name change meeting, 604
  Perverted pulpit message, ix
  Satan's lair, 568
  Summer (1992), 599
  Theft, 141
  Theft & the Court, 960
  Theft details, 608
  Theft, AFCM tried to hide, 612
  Theft, authorities ignored, 595
  Theft, eight events, 602
Sorcerers, 38, 417
Sorrow, 679
  See Thoughts
Soul
  Between spirit and body, 420
  Can be killed, 420
  Can choose death, 420
  Departs at death of body, 419
  Graphic, your earthly essence, 427
  Lacking, 81
  Lying destroys, 897
  No neutral observer, 432
  Nothing on earth worth, 590

Index

Souls
    Belong to God, 29, 410
    For Satan, 398
    Lost, 453
    Who sin shall die, 411
Soul-Spirit Life
    God's design, graphic, 522
    In Satan's world, 523
    In world with Holy Spirit, 524
Sow, Reap, 442
Speaks
    Bible To heart, 20
Spirit
    How automatic pilot works, 642
    Testifies to our spirit, 433
Spirit of Antichrist
    Denies humanity of Christ, 466
Spirit of Christ, 73
Spirit of God, 73
Spirit of Truth
    In action, 21
    One of God's seven Spirits, 303
    Via Christ in abundance, viii
Spirit-Soul Force
    Discussion & graphic, 421
Spirit-Soul-Body
    Whole, graphic, 419
Spiritual
    Armor, 422
    Birth required, for kingdom, 1029
    Blind leaders, 619
    Ecstasy, 881
    Fifteen Church warnings, 580
    Food, 590
    Gifts, 552
    Influence, 573
    Intelligent quotient, 379
    Irony, 752
    Man's responsibility to God, 551
    Ministries, 566
    Myopic vision, 560
    Pastor's power play, 568
    Political policies v. weight, 995
    Violence, 989
Spiritual Forces
    Graphic, 140
    Two fundamental forces, 140
Spiritual Influence
    Christianity, 471
    Phase 1 - God's fellowship, 462
    Phase 2 - Man sins, 464
    Phase 3 - Satan wins, 465
    Phase 4 - Christ's humanity, 467
    Phase 5 - Spirit of Truth sent, 469
    Strength graph by phases, 470
    Summary Table, 471
Spiritual Journey
    Edward's, 419
Spiritual, Oneness, 300
Spiritual, Two
    Choices, 168
    Destinations, 168
    Directions, 168
    Paths, 168
    People, 168
    Tools, 168
    Turfs, 168
Standard
    Behavior, 641
Standup, For Word
    Demonstrates understanding, 194
Stanley, Charles, 325
    Apostate teachings, 185
    False doctrines, 190
    Trinity, 243
Stem Cells, 730
Steps
    God directs man's, 75
Stewardship, 82
Still, Be
    Know God, 251
Straight Ways, 35
Stress, 497, 501
    Three ways to deal with, 502
Stroud, Elizabeth
    Methodist Lesbian Minister, 986

Index

Study, 95
Stumble, 142
Stupid, 172
Submit, 483
Submitting, 354
Suffer, 322
   Real believers will, 440
Suffering For Christ, 439
Suicide, God did not commit, 128
Summation
   Law and prophets, 633
Surrender, 132
Surrendered, 12, 418
Swaggart, Jimmy, 774
Swindler, 545
Sword, 590
Tail, 4
Talk v. Walk, 29
Talk, Empty, 897
Talking To God, 120
Talmud, 367
Tanakh, 367
Teach
   The Law, 582
Teacher
   Commissioned by God, 110
   Higher standard, 329
Teachers, False
   Nine facts from Jesus, 563
Teaching
   Watch closely, 416
Teaching Ability
   God gave Bezaleel, 171
Teachings
   Tested against Scripture, 94
Temple, 17
   Defiles, 17
Temptation, 443, 823
Ten Commandments, 19
   Christ enhanced, 136
   Obeying them, 186
   v. Good citizen, 185
   You can't obey them? 185

Terror, 61, 946, 947
Testimony
   Witnesses, 2-3, 64
Tetragrammaton, 310
Theft
   Elk River Assembly of God, 546
   Solid Rock Church, 4
Thieves, 38
Thinking, Critical, 778
Thought-Action Process
   Normal, 762
   Sexually Immoral, 762
   Spiritually enhanced, 762
Thoughts, 57
   Choices from heart, 156
   Feel good, do it? 760
   Focus on positive, Philip 4:8, 786
   God's are higher, 198
   Mind v. heart graphic, 695
   Random, 786
   Self-contained graphic, 763
   Sources with God, graphic, 758
   Sources without God, graphic, 759
   Then actions, then emotions, 761
   Transcending sorrow, 384
   Transcends, 423
   Wondrous, 573
Tithe
   29 Instructions in Word, 620
   Advance to Malachi 3:16, 665
   Based on increase, formula, 669
   Business gross lie, 670
   Can't meet need perversion, 670
   Christ was a poor man, 661
   Christ's death cancelled, 664
   Christian mythology, 618
   Cursed? 625
   Designed for worship, food, 618
   Extortioners & liars, 673
   Five simple facts, 668
   Free will offerings built Temple, 662
   God defined, you can't redefine, 1042
   Graphic of instructions, 622

Copyright 2005 Edward G. Palmer, All Rights Reserved.

Index

Tithe (Continued)
   Gross blessing or gross lie, 669
   Instructions not open to change, 619
   Jesus says, "It is written," 672
   Jesus speaks, 616
   Jewish Rabbis know better, 662
   Lawlessness connection, 623
   Levites provided services, 663
   List of five food attributes, 667
   Malachi only about food, 667
   Malachi perverted, 665
   Message of Satan, 677
   Message used by Satan, 660
   Ministers, rich, 661
   No one out gives God, 671
   Only two types of income tithed, 662
   Part of ceremonial laws, 625
   Part of law, 618
   Preachers, 629
   Programming, 618
   Robbers identified, 663
   Salaried gross lie, 671
   The Tithing Dilemma, 661
   Ultimate perversion, Matthews, 666
   v. God's Word and liars, 676
   Warning to teachers of, 677
   Word of Faith, 616
   See Giving; Matthews, William
Tithe Law, 615
Tithe, Modern Teaching
   Abomination to God, 418
Tithers
   Cursed by tithing, irony, 628
Tithing
   Anxiety, 674
   God doesn't need your money, 675
   Living under ceremonial laws, 628
Tongues, 535, 553
   Salvation debate, 554
   Whole congregation, 553
Torah, 367
Tradition
   Purgatory, 278
   v. God's commands, 14
   See Trinity Doctrine
Tradition Negating God, 457
Traditions, 13
   Man-made, 14
Transfiguration, 207
Transgress, 13
Traumatized, 61
Trials, 500
   Earthly, 7
Tribulations
   To enter kingdom, 1029
Trinity
   False doctrine, 181
   NKJV graphic, 98
   Not found in Bible, 255
   Rationalization of sin, 130
Trinity Believer, 458
Trinity Doctrine
   Alpha & Omega, 266
   Alpha & Omega Analysis, 287
   Believer goes to heaven? 494
   Bible doesn't support, 276
   Bible verse summary table, 276
   Billy Graham, 310
   Christians created it, 257
   From Antichrist, 307
   God exists in three subsistences, 255
   Hagee, the best explanation, 258
   I and Father are one analysis, 293
   Implications, Jack Miles', 289
   Interlocking fish graphic, 254
   Interlocking sixes graphic, 254
   Makes Jesus God, 190
   Morphs Jesus into God, 214
   Not supported by Scripture, 278
   Offensive to God, 980
   Orthodox Christianity, 255
   Paradise statement one reason, 283
   Pray to Jesus? 280
   Rationalization, 205
   Rationalization by Jack Miles, 211
   Rationalizes man's desire to sin, 214

Index

Trinity Doctrine (Continued)
   Scripture analysis, 258
   Supported by tradition only, 278
   Symbol, 252
   Symbol, NKJV, 253
   Teaches idolatry, 309
   Three co-equal parts, 252
   v. Word of God, 242
   See Hagee, John
Trinity v. Word
   Antichrist, 307
   Attributes of God and Jesus, 302
   Christ ascends to God, 245
   God greater than all, 245
   God greater than Jesus, 245
   God has seven Spirits, 265
   God took Enoch, 286
   Jesus "made" like all men, 291
   One flesh analysis, 296
   One with God, us, 298
   Scripture against trinity, table, 305
   Seven Spirits, 301
True Love
   In heart v. mind, 435
Trust
   Entire Bible, 23
Truth
   Definition, 223
   Ferret out, 94
   Five step process, 219
   God not in lies, 9
   Not welcomed, 685
   Perverted at the pulpit, ix
   Second place to dogma, 457
   Taking a stand, 5
   Those who know are called, 26
   Turning back on, 9, 593
Truth Squad, 97
Turf, Four Zones
   Defined, graphic, 164
   Discussed, 165
Turf, God
   Defined, 148

Turf, Righteous, 108
Turf, Satan
   Defined, 148
   Discussion, 149
Turf, Two in Life
   Defined, 147
Turf, Unrighteous, 108
Turn and live, 33
Turnabout
   180 Degrees, 30
Unchaste, 807
Understanding
   Target graphic, 182
   Target graphic, 183
   Comes from committed heart, 174
   Comes from interacting, 176
   Target graphic, 184
   Daniel's, of dream, 176
   Don't lean on your own, 82
   Exoteric graphic, 189
   God gave Bezaleel, 171
   God gave Solomon, 171
   God opened their minds, 203
   God's breath gives us, 200
   Heart v. Mind, 757
   In heart, 201
   Is to depart from evil, 171
   Jesus is not God, 195
   Jesus is Son, not God, 196
   Jesus speaks for God, 195
   Lack of, 26
   Lean not on your own, 198
   Paradox, 197
   Requires dedicated heart, 189
   Seven keys to God's Word, 203
   Twelve biblical facts, 200
Understanding of God
   Jesus gave us, 171, 415
Unfit to Teach, 677
Ungodly, 38
Unintended Events, 687
Union Church, 548, 552

Index

United States
    Biblical message for, 968
    Faces a new moral war, 969
    Formed as Christian nation, 943
    Founded on Bible & Christianity, 953
    History of people of faith, 945
    Made a covenant with God, 943
    Moral nation? 235
    Moral unity, commingling, 948
    Once faithful to God, 941
    Reaping what it sowed, terror, 946
    Rebelling against God, 943
    Society has upside down mores, 985
    Used to submit to God, 355
Unnerving, 60
Unrighteous, 38
    Close to Satan, 107
    Don't compare to righteous, 1034
    God's penalty pursues, 968
    See Hill, Paul J
Unwed Mother, 727
Vegetative State, 508
Vengeance, 54
    Belongs to God, 349
    On God's schedule, 349
Vessel, 808
    Paul chosen, 31
Vessel, Earthly
    Shedding, 439
Virginity, 640
Virtue, 951
Voters, Black, 10
Wages of Sin, Death, 413
Walk In Spirit, Start
    Discussion & graphic, 424
Walk In The Spirit, 759
Walk with God
    Graphic, 43
Walking In Flesh
    Graphic, 425
Walking In Spirit
    Graphic, 425
Walking With God, 109

Walsch, Neale Donald
    Conversations With God, 980
Warning
    Don't teach sexual immorality, 896
    Don't treat Jesus as God, 588
    FDA & pharmaceuticals attack, 541
    Fifteen Church, 580
    First love [God], 587
    Pubic rebuke, 592
    Tithe teachers, 677
    To abortion supporters, 748
    To Christians, ix
    To couples cohabitating, 837
    To immoral teachers, 1038
    To repent, from Jesus, 51
    Voting against God, teaching, 976
Warriors, 4
    Salvation, 99
Washington, George, 942
Wedding Ring
    Edward's, 434
Weighed, 89
Weight
    Opinions, God v. men, 65
Weightier, 627
White, Barry (song), 877
Whole Heart
    Search with, 177
    Required, 27
Wickedness
    Pastor's, 68
Wide Path
    Discussion, 162
Wide Path, Destruction
    Defined, graphic, 151
Wifey, 799
Willful
    Sinner, 41
Willful Sin, Bad Habits, 516
Willful Sin, End to
    Blood plus Spirit, 373

Index

Willful Sinners
   Don't belong in church, 46
   Don't keep company with, 46
   Unrepentant people, 46
Wisdom, 21, 197
   Basic steps to, 752
   Connotes knowledge, 758
   God gave Bezaleel, 171
   Heart v. mind, 757
   In mind, 201
   James speaks, 454
   Yields to reason, 454
   See Fear of LORD
Wise
   Doers of word, 997
Witness, 593
Woe
   Abortionites, 946
   Sanctioning homosexual clergy, 857
   Shedding innocent blood, 946
   To judges that fine the innocent, 966
   To porn promoters, 803
   To uncaring pastors, 995
Woes, 791
WOF Church, 579
   Clocking pew hours v. word, 583
   Designed to feed itching ears, 590
   Easy to spot, 581
   Feeds emotions, hides apostasy, 589
   Ignorant of Malachi 3:16, 584
   Knows Malachi 3:8, 584
   Moneychangers, modern day, 582
Wolves, 975
Womb, 711
   Fruit of, from God, 725
   Leah's opened, 724
Word
   Don't add to or subtract from, 1042
   Faith, hope & love in it, 1039
   Must take priority over church, 1042
   Supreme, in your life, 244
Word of Faith
   Counterfeit church, 579
   False teachings, 621
   False tithe teaching, 616
   Give to get message, 660
   See WOF Church
Works, 4
   Defines faith, 998
   Justified Rahab, 87
Works of Flesh, 96
Works, Greater
   Than Jesus', 418
World
   Opposite of God's interests, 316
World War II, 78
Worries, 500
Worship
   Becomes a daily act, 653
   By killing, false, 678
   Christ is our priest, 126
   Christ says God only, 126
   Duty, John Adams, 951
   God, 7
   God alone, 1013
   God asks Christ, did you teach, 1012
   In Spirit and Truth, 228
   Lifting up hands, 552
   Only God, 371
   Praise, 17
   The Father, 7
   True, involves emotions, 576
   Vain, 395
   Vain and useless, ix
Worshipped, 315
Worshipping God
   In vain, ix
   Wonderful, viii
Wrath
   Awaits sinners, 69
Yahweh, 137
YHWH, *See* Tetragrammaton
Zealot, 71

JVED Publishing

18140 Zane Street NW #410
Elk River, Minnesota 55330

www.jvedpublishing.org

Special Acknowledgements

The Apostle Edward would like to thank Dean and Jackie Mattila along with Vernon Enstad for their spiritual and emotional support during his four plus years of writing. Without their godly personal support and input, this work for God may not have been possible. This book was a spiritual journey for all four of them. A special thanks is also due Brian Mechler for his proof reading assistance. Book updates and errata data will be posted online at http://www.edwardtheapostle.org. For people in countries where the book is not available in print form or for those who prefer, it may be read and searched free online in English via web browsers at this web site.

The Apostle Edward asks ...
Are You Ready?

When he returns for souls, will Christ find you going about God's business? Will he find your spiritual light shining? If not, why? Do you even know why Christ stated those two salvation requirements?

There is an exodus from established churches by Christians who have found out that many churches no longer teach God's truth. The trend is worldwide and was the subject of a recent newsletter I received. These Christians read the Bible and compared what their church taught. They found that the Church supported many evil things that God abhors. In the process, they have asked themselves some fundamental spiritual questions:

- Can we support abortion if God abhors the shedding of innocent blood?
- Can we support Gay rights if God says homosexuality is abominable?
- Can we support a political party that seeks to excise God from everyday life?
- Can we support world friendship when it makes us His enemy?

Christian mythology is rampant. The Book of Edward discusses the above and many other important issues that the Church is now confronted with. Will you personally obey God's Word and the teachings of Jesus? If not, you are not saved. This book can reawaken your spirit and save your soul. At the very least, it will educate your heart.

I can remember the first experience in which I felt betrayed and confused by a pulpit teaching that did not line up and match what the word of God actually said. The basic choice you have, as a Christian, is whether you will adhere to God's Word or to the man made doctrines of your social group, your church, its hierarchy or its denomination.

There lies the main issue of salvation. You'll have to decide on God's Word if you want eternal life for in the end analysis you will be held accountable to His Word. Christians are leaving the established church and finding small fellowships or home churches as described in the New Testament. God has opened their eyes to His truth and if you read and study the Scriptures in this book, He will open your eyes.

If desired, you may write to me in care of JVED Publishing. May your soul find the true salvation contained in the teachings of Jesus Christ. The Apostle Edward

www.ingramcontent.com/pod-product-compliance
Lightning Source LLC
Chambersburg PA
CBHW082120230426
43671CB00015B/2752